RIVERS OF CU

A Canoeists Guide

RIVERS OF CUMBRIA

By Mike Hayward

Published by CORDEE Leicester

© Mike Hayward, Cordee 1992
First published 1988
Second Edition 1992

Hayward, Mike
  Rivers of Cumbria : a guide for canoeists.
  1. Canoes and canoeing——England——
  Cumbria——Handbooks, manuals, etc.
  I. Title
  914.27'804858'0247971   GV776.44.C8/

  ISBN 1 871890 36 5

BDS CS7

Front Cover Photo: Robin Evringham on the river Lune, just above the narrow slot (section G in guide) at low water levels.

Printed by: Joseph Ward (Printers) Ltd, Dewsbury, West Yorkshire.

This guidebook is available from all specialist equipment shops, and some book shops within the area. It can be obtained direct from the publishers, together with most other books for canoeists. Write for a copy of our comprehensive stocklist of outdoor recreation and travel books/maps.

CORDEE
3a De Montfort Street, Leicester, LE1 7HD

Contents

Acknowledgements

I would like to thank all those canoeists who have paddled with me in Cumbria and enabled me to gain the knowledge that has allowed the compiling of this guide. Especially – Steve Bate, Chris Lockyer and Gareth Walker.

Introduction

All the rivers in this guide can be found in Cumbria and North Lancashire; some are easy, others more difficult. At low levels the smaller rivers offer no more than a trickle, more appropriate to wellies than a canoe. But in spate they can offer canoeing as exciting and difficult as anywhere else in the country.

The rivers can be roughly divided into three sorts: those fed by lakes, those longer rivers which can be canoed at all levels, and those which are only canoeable in flood conditions after heavy rainfall.

I have tried to include an indication for each river which will tell you if it is likely to be possible to canoe it.

A general warning: low branches and fallen trees can often cause problems on the smaller rivers.

It is likely that the rivers can be in condition at any time of year owing to the peculiarities of the Cumbrian climate.

This guide is intended only to offer advice and information about each river and its nature. It should be used as such, not as a bible. There is no substitute for an on-the-spot analysis of each situation. If you are in any doubt, inspect each section of river before you canoe it.

SPECIAL NOTE

Please note that the information in this book is correct at the time of going to press. The situation as to access to and from rivers is particularly variable.

Neither the possession of this book, nor the information it contains, gives anyone the right to canoe on any of the rivers mentioned.

Using the guide

Each river in this guide has a map and associated written text, which in some cases includes a more detailed map of some of the rapids and falls. The grade given to a river is its overall grade. For example, a grade II with one grade III section would be graded at II with a note about the grade III section. However, five or six grade III sections would gain it a grade III.

The rivers are graded at 'normal' canoeing levels, not necessarily when it is at a bank high flood. Some rivers become very technical requiring precise steering at low levels, and becoming washed out in flood. Others develop serious stoppers and large waves in flood conditions. The grades do not take this into account. In flood a steady grade III with breakouts can become a fast-flowing deluge with few breakouts, but the increased volume of water would not necessarily make it a grade IV, although it would be a more committing river.

At the end of the guide a short description of some of the less well known rivers and becks is given.

The section on access is correct at the time of going to print, but can always change. *You* are asked to observe all access agreements as they stand.

The timings given are for a group of fit and competent canoeists doing a run down the river without playing. A large group with novices could expect to double or treble these times.

The maps

Each map has been kept simple but is designed to include enough detail for you to be able to find your place on a river.

The letters on the side of the map relate directly across to the river – this has been done to avoid complicating the drawings.

A letter such as this   A letter such as this

will refer to a section of   will refer to a specific point
the river giving a general   on the river, such as a fall
description.   or weir.

The description for each river is set out to correspond with the letters on each map. In the description each section of the river is given an overall grade, followed by the description for that section. For example:

A(II) would mean section A was grade II

─A(W) would mean section A was a weir

─A(F) would mean section A was a large waterfall

─A(V) would mean section A was a grade V rapid

Key to the maps

River		additional features on detailed drawings	
Weir		Prominent boulder	●
Footbridge		Overhanging trees	
Motorway/dual carriageway		Suggested route	
A road		Flow of river	
B road		Shingle bank	
Railway		Tree in river	⊙
Disused railway		Stopper wave	
Built-up area		Line of trees	× × × × ×
Wooded area		Rocky ridge	
Telephone	T	Standing waves	
Car park	P	Prominent building	
Telegraph wires/ power lines			
Side stream			

River grading

Grade I   Flat water. Generally slow-flowing sections broken by small waves. You should be able to float down with no problems.

Grade II   Faster-flowing water, with rocks which need to be avoided. Small waves, with obvious large eddy pools. Some larger regular waves. There is normally a choice of routes.

Grade III   Larger waves, faster water, some tight breakouts. Rocks cause broken and some confused water. Some stoppers are found. The route is usually easily seen. Flat sections usually found between rapids. There is a need to have full control of your craft. Inspection advised.

Grade IV   More continuous rapids with large waves. Stoppers will hold a boat. Route not easily distinguished. Breakouts few and small. Will require precise control and good decision making for a successful descent. There is difficulty in picking out features of the chosen route whilst on the water. Inspection is advised. Boat can easily be trapped on obstructions. Also narrow gorges with several falls in quick succession.

Grade V   All of grade IV taken to the extreme. Continuous large rapids with irregular stoppers and waves. The planning of a route is difficult due to the ever-changing water. A swim would be serious. Inspection usually essential.

Grade VI   Not found in Cumbria.

Grade F   The loopy grade where bottle is usually of more consequence than skill. A small mistake could be disastrous – waterfalls and some weirs.

NB No attempt has been made to grade any weir mentioned in this guide. A weir may be easy to shoot or impossible. Each should be respected for what it is.

RIVERS OF CUMBRIA

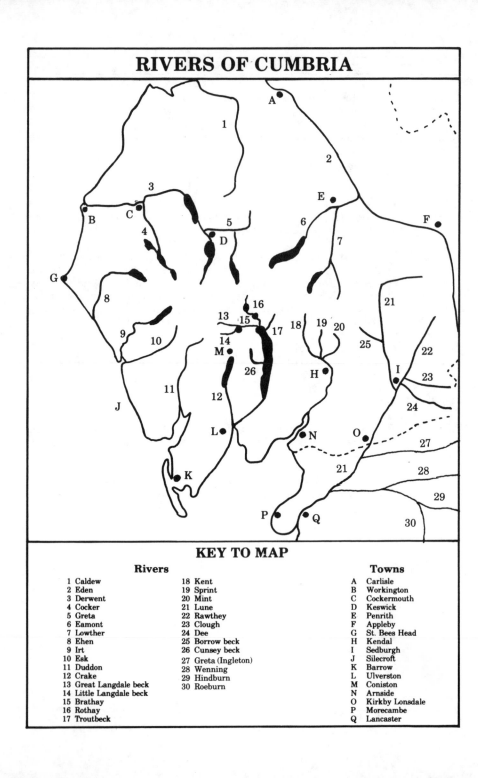

KEY TO MAP

Rivers

1	Caldew	
2	Eden	
3	Derwent	
4	Cocker	
5	Greta	
6	Eamont	
7	Lowther	
8	Ehen	
9	Irt	
10	Esk	
11	Duddon	
12	Crake	
13	Great Langdale beck	
14	Little Langdale beck	
15	Brathay	
16	Rothay	
17	Troutbeck	
18	Kent	
19	Sprint	
20	Mint	
21	Lune	
22	Rawthey	
23	Clough	
24	Dee	
25	Borrow beck	
26	Cunsey beck	
27	Greta (Ingleton)	
28	Wenning	
29	Hindburn	
30	Roeburn	

Towns

A	Carlisle
B	Workington
C	Cockermouth
D	Keswick
E	Penrith
F	Appleby
G	St. Bees Head
H	Kendal
I	Sedburgh
J	Silecroft
K	Barrow
L	Ulverston
M	Coniston
N	Arnside
O	Kirkby Lonsdale
P	Morecambe
Q	Lancaster

RIVER BRATHAY

GRADE: Elter water – Skelwith force I
Skelwith force – Skelwith bridge (F) Portage then III
Skelwith bridge – Windermere I then II

TIME: 2 hours or more

DETAILS: LENGTH 4km   HEIGHT LOSS 20m   GRADIENT 5m/km

INDICATOR: In the field at G.R. 358.036 is a large pond, separated from the river by a reed bed. If there is an obvious water connection between the pond and the river, then the river will be at a reasonable height. In flood, most of the field is covered with water.

ACCESS:

Car park in Elterwater village	328.047
Skelwith force	341.044
'Muddy' layby	352.035
Brathay footbridge	363.034
Brathay pool	366.034
North end of lake Windermere	376.033

NB There is no longer access to the river at Skelwith bridge, as canoeists have annoyed the landowners and a fence has been erected.

GENERAL DESCRIPTION

The river Brathay is often paddled by novice groups from the 'muddy' layby to Brathay pool. Skelwith force (a waterfall of about 3.5m) attracts thousands of visitors each year. Several canoeists have lost their lives from shooting the falls in error. The section from Brathay footbridge to Brathay pool is probably the most canoed stretch of water in Cumbria. Ambleside Area Adventure Association sometimes erect slalom poles on the river, above or below Brathay pool. If the river is combined with Great Langdale beck an excellent day out is to be had.

DESCRIPTION

A(II) Access to Elter water is difficult. It is better to get on the bottom section of Great Langdale beck in Elterwater village, where car parking is available adjacent to the river. An easy but fast stretch leads directly to Elter water.

B(I) The Brathay starts as it flows out of Elter water. A twisting flat section leads to a sign in the river near the left bank. This sign warns of the waterfall below. PORTAGE on the left bank to below Skelwith force.

C(F) The falls have been shot successfully by a few loopy enthusiasts. The approach is to the left of a rocky island below the sign in the river. A stopper, which forms on a small broken weir and is large enough to stop you and deviate you from your chosen route, forms about 20m above the falls. The river needs to be quite high for you to shoot the falls successfully, as at low levels the water crashes on to rocks, half-way down the falls on the right-hand side. These falls can be *terminal* and should not be taken lightly. The falls plunge into a deep pool full of aerated water, which would be very nasty for a swimmer. The outflow from the pool is a small drop, with a playful stopper. If the river is in flood you will be able to loop and do popouts in this stopper. Note, this is not the stopper at the base of the falls itself.

D(III)   After your portage to below the falls the next section could cause you some problems. Several lines of trees, large waves and rocks add to the interest. This section is difficult to inspect properly. The first stretch is best tackled via the right-hand route. Both the left and central routes will necessitate a manoeuvre through lines of trees, if you can find a gap. A more open stretch on a rock-strewn bend where the river is quite wide leads to a second route-choice between lines of trees. The left or central lines are the best. The trees finish above Skelwith bridge.

E(I)   Below Skelwith bridge the river is calmer. The road nears the left bank, where the 'muddy' layby can be found. A few hundred metres lead to a house on the left with two stone lions in its garden. In flood conditions the lions have only their heads showing above the water. More flat water follows.

F(II)   The flow now quickens and both banks are lined by thick bushes. A big eddy pool on the right provides a spot to rest before the descent to Brathay footbridge. Below the footbridge is a good place to practise ferry glides. The National Trust are keen to keep erosion of the river banks to a minimum around the footbridge: please take note of any signs. Another 250m down the river is a short rapid, normally grade II, but III in spate conditions. Below is Brathay pool which will catch swimmers, boats, etc. Parking is available next to this pool.

G(II)   At the outlet of the pool is a wooded island, which becomes covered in flood; this is best passed on the left. More small rapids and then flat water lead to the confluence with the river Rothay, and on to lake Windermere.

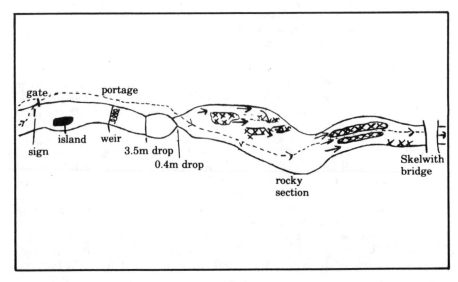

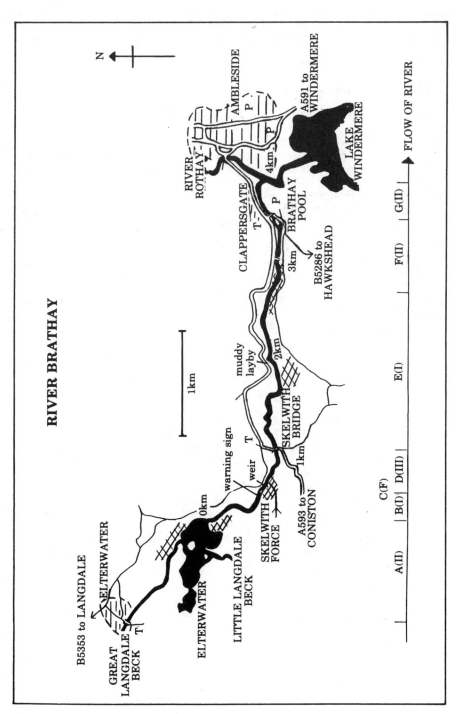

RIVER BRATHAY

N

B5353 to LANGDALE

GREAT LANGDALE BECK

ELTERWATER

ELTERWATER

LITTLE LANGDALE BECK

SKELWITH FORCE

A593 to CONISTON

SKELWITH BRIDGE

warning sign

weir

muddy layby

0km

1km

2km

3km

4km

B5286 to HAWKSHEAD

BRATHAY POOL

CLAPPERSGATE

RIVER ROTHAY

AMBLESIDE

A591 to WINDERMERE

LAKE WINDERMERE

1km

FLOW OF RIVER

A(II)   B(I) D(III)   E(I)   F(II)   G(II)

C(F)

3

RIVER COCKER

GRADE: II with some III at the end

TIME: 2 hours or more

DETAILS: LENGTH 11km   HEIGHT LOSS 58m GRADIENT 5.3m/km

INDICATOR: It is best to look at the river from one of the bridges in Cockermouth, in order to get an idea of the level of water. At low water many small rocks are obvious, these being covered after periods of rain.

ACCESS:

Minor road bridge	148.213
Southwaite bridge	130.283
Bridge on the river Derwent	116.306

GENERAL DESCRIPTION

The Cocker drains Crummock water, and flows into the river Derwent in Cockermouth. It holds a good level of water even a few days after heavy rain since it is fed by Crummock water, which in turn is supplied by Buttermere and Loweswater. Much of the upper part above Southwaite bridge is flat, and often has a number of trees completely blocking the river. The main interest is as the river flows through Cockermouth.

DESCRIPTION

A(W)   A small weir near a small parking place provides a good place to start the river. This is only a few hundred metres from the outflow from the lake.

B(I/II)   In flood the water is fast and trees can cause problems, as mentioned above. On a series of tight bends the water is more difficult with standing waves. No further difficulties should be found until you pass under Southwaite bridge. (There is a possibility of fences spanning the river, but they are often washed away by flood water.) From Southwaite bridge several bends lead to a small wooded island; this is passed to the left, where standing waves will be found. Shortly after this you pass under the new road bridge and around a loop in the river.

C(II/III)   On the loop a sharp right bend leads you into standing waves and stoppers. From here you pass down through the town on a series of rapids, some easy, others requiring more care. There are several footbridges across the river but none provides an easy egress point. It is better to continue on down to the river Derwent and egress on the right bank above the road bridge.

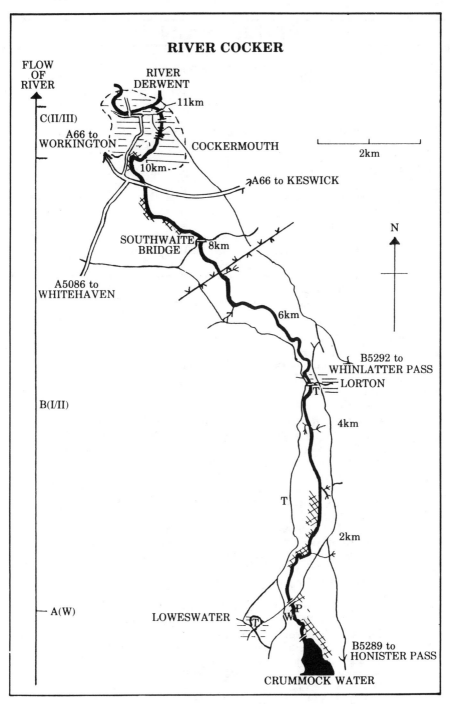

RIVER COCKER

FLOW
OF
RIVER

C(II/III)

RIVER
DERWENT

11km

A66 to
WORKINGTON

COCKERMOUTH

2km

10km

A66 to KESWICK

N

SOUTHWAITE
BRIDGE

8km

A5086 to
WHITEHAVEN

6km

B5292 to
WHINLATTER PASS
LORTON

T

B(I/II)

4km

T

2km

A(W)

LOWESWATER

T

P
W

B5289 to
HONISTER PASS

CRUMMOCK WATER

5

RIVER CRAKE

GRADE: II with two sections of III. No portages

TIME: 2½ hours or more for the full trip

DETAILS: LENGTH 8km   HEIGHT LOSS 48m   GRADIENT 6m/km

INDICATOR: The clearance of the bridge at Spark bridge is about 1.5m at low levels.

ACCESS: Public parking at Brown Howe on the west side of Coniston
water   291.111
or Blawith common   287.901
Spark bridge (west bank below the bridge)   .   306.849
Greenodd (north side of the river) – see map   316.826
Permission should be sought to park at the garage in Greenodd.
Inspection of the Bobbin Mill rapid section I is not permitted from either bank.
Large groups should avoid finishing at Spark Bridge.

GENERAL DESCRIPTION

Most of the river is flat broken by a mixture of man-made and natural obstructions. These provide small but frequent waves and rapids. Thick bushes line the banks in many places. At low levels the river can be a scrape; but in spate, it provides a swift and exciting run.

DESCRIPTION

A(I)   Access from the car park on Blawith common needs a portage of about 300m to the lake shore. The car park at Brown Howe is on the lake shore, but will require a longer paddle to the start of the river. The end of the lake is lined by reeds, where the flow quickens to Allan tarn, a large, still pool.

B(II)   Downstream from Allan tarn the river proper starts. The first section has bushes on either side, and leads to Bouthray bridge, which provides the first real breakouts. This is followed by an S-bend with eddy pools; a few hundred metres on is a sharp left bend.

C(III)   The first of the grade III rapids (about 50m long). This rapid can be inspected from the right bank, which is wooded. The weir at the top can be shot anywhere but usually right of centre. The main flow follows a twisting course; at high levels breakouts on the right are difficult to make. There are many rocks, and the less experienced paddler will have difficulty in doing any more than simply running the rapid, normally getting pushed on to rocks on the left, half-way down, unless some avoiding action is taken. There are several eddies at the bottom of the rapid. The next section is grade II with plenty of rocks.

D(W)   A small weir follows immediately. This will hold a boat presented sideways on, but rescue is not difficult.

E(II)   An easier section follows, with many large eddies. Trees line and overhang the left bank. You will also pass under a footbridge.

6

F(II)	A low easy-angled weir should present no problems, though the left side is broken and a strand of barbed wire hangs menacingly on the left bank. Easy water leads to another weir, also low, which can be taken anywhere. There is a strong tow to the right, as the weir is angled across the river. Lowick bridge is just below.
G(II)	Below Lowick bridge the flow quickens. Two islands are passed on the left. At the first island the main flow is to the right, but this course will lead to considerable problems with trees. The left channel is narrower but safe. After the second island there follows a kilometre of swifter flow and pleasant rapids with some larger waves. This section ends with a weir.
H(W)	This weir has a drop of just over 1m. It is normally taken in the centre, but at low levels 2m from the left bank is best. Several boats have met their end impaled on sharp rocks and spikes on this weir, so *take care.*
I(III)	Around the next corner is the Bobbin mill rapid, guarded by a large sloping weir. This is normally taken on the left easier-angled side. The weir is followed by rough water, which leads to a footbridge with small breakouts immediately downstream. The bottom section is steep, with several small stoppers, which should cause no problems. At the bottom of the rapid, overhanging branches on the left bank could cause problems. These can be avoided by making a difficult breakout, in an eddy, that forms behind rocks in the middle of the river, at the bottom of the rapid.
J(II)	100m downstream is Spark bridge, which can be difficult in flood conditions because of a lack of air space. Spark bridge is a good place to stop, and many groups choose to finish their trip here. On downstream is an island which should be passed on the left.
K(W)	The next obstacle of any consequence is a weir constructed from boulders. It has a drop of 1m, and can be safely negotiated in several places.
L(I)	The flow now slackens considerably and the final kilometre is of flat water, which leads under Penny bridge to the sea.
M(W)	The final trick of the river is yet another weir, situated just upstream from Greenodd bridge. This weir has a strong towback, and has been known to eat canoes. At high tide the weir disappears, but on the ebb tide the towback on the stopper of the weir increases. If you should happen to get stuck in the weir, perhaps all you need do is wait for high tide.

For the enthusiast Morecambe bay is beyond, or you can leave the river on the bank below the road bridge (see plan).

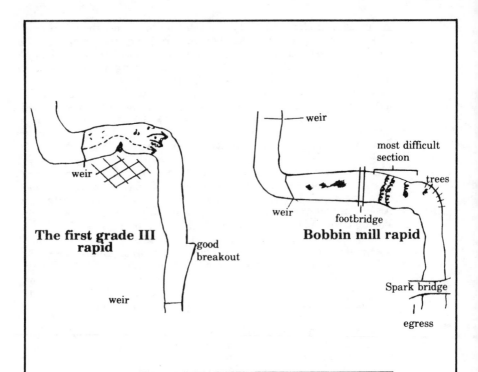

The first grade III rapid

Bobbin mill rapid

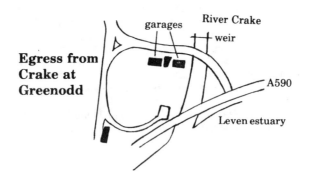

Egress from Crake at Greenodd

RIVER CRAKE

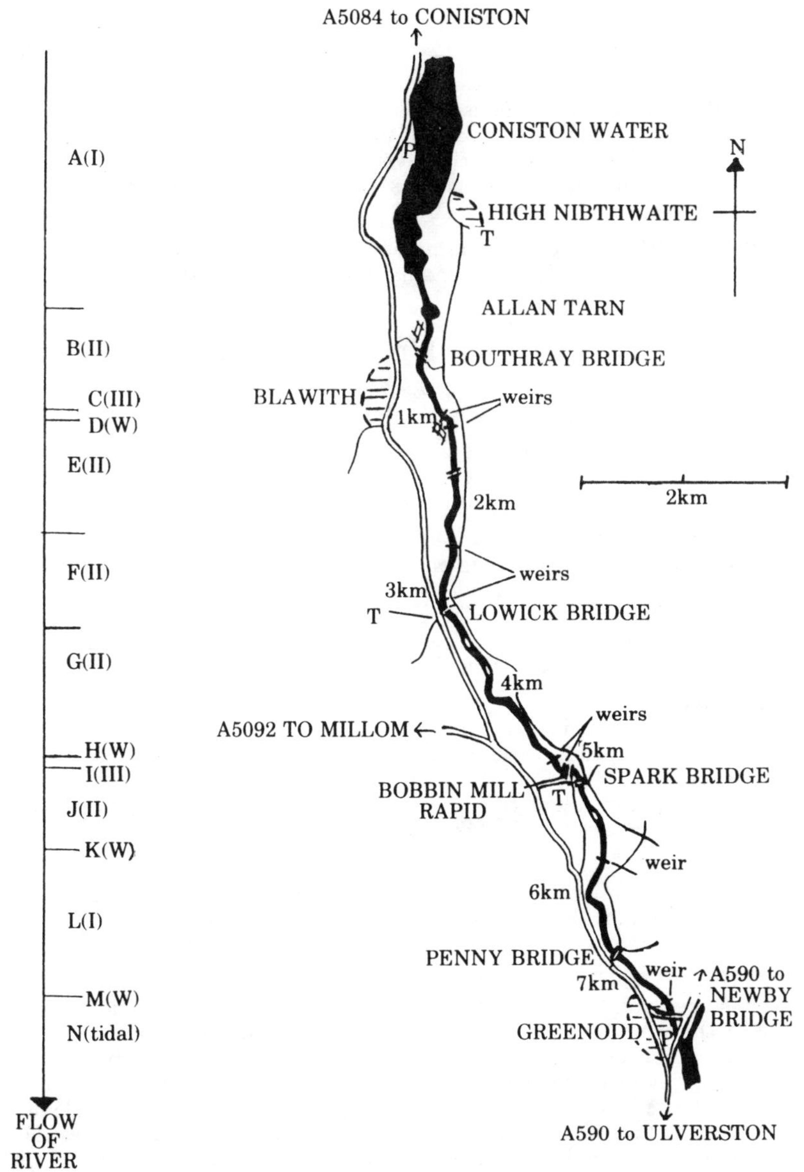

A5084 to CONISTON

CONISTON WATER

A(I)

N

HIGH NIBTHWAITE
T

P

ALLAN TARN

B(II)

BOUTHRAY BRIDGE

C(III)
D(W)

BLAWITH

weirs

1km

E(II)

2km

2km

F(II)

weirs

3km

LOWICK BRIDGE

T

G(II)

4km

weirs

H(W)

A5092 TO MILLOM ←

5km

I(III)

SPARK BRIDGE

J(II)

BOBBIN MILL
RAPID

T

K(W)

weir

6km

L(I)

PENNY BRIDGE

weir

A590 to

7km

NEWBY

M(W)

BRIDGE

N(tidal)

GREENODD

FLOW
OF
RIVER

A590 to ULVERSTON

RIVER DERWENT

GRADE: I and II

TIME: Upper 1 hour Middle ½ hour Lower 3 hours

DETAILS:

	LENGTH	HEIGHT LOSS	GRADIENT
Upper	8km	25m	3.1m/km
Middle	4km	9m	2.25m/km
Lower	13km	30m	2.4m/km

INDICATOR: The upper section is best indicated at Grange bridge, where there are large pebbly banks. If there is an obvious deep route between the shingle banks the river will be deep enough to canoe. The middle and lower sections are paddleable at most times of the year.

ACCESS:

Upper There are numerous places to start along the side of the B5289, the main problem being finding somewhere to park.
Grange bridge 253.175
The shores of Derwent water

Middle The shores of Derwent water
Small bridge 236.268

Lower Ouse bridge 200.321
Road bridge 163.333
Cockermouth bridge 116.306

GENERAL DESCRIPTION
The Derwent flows from Borrowdale into Derwent water, and then as it flows out of this lake it is joined by the Greta and flows into Bassenthwaite lake. From this lake it flows west to Cockermouth where it is joined by the Cocker, before the long section to the sea at Workington. It is rarely canoed in its entirety as the two lakes involve long paddles of nearly 5km and 6km respectively.

DESCRIPTION
A(II) Above the confluence with Stonethwaite beck the river is rarely deep enough to paddle. The rapids are small and well spaced, the scenery is excellent.

B(I) The last few kilometres are very flat. A footbridge gives an indication of the approach of the lake.

Middle (I/II)
There are many trees lining both banks. The waves are caused in the main by shallow shingle banks. Do not pass the last bridge unless you intend to paddle across Bassenthwaite.

Lower (I/II)
The river is easy and wide. There are a lot of parts with small standing waves. The first of the weirs is now demolished but care should be taken to avoid the spikes that remain. The best egress point is the right bank upstream of the road bridge in Cockermouth. The weir around the bend from this bridge is now broken. It can be recognized from above by a large lump of concrete in the middle of the river. The left side provides the easiest route through the standing waves. There is no easy access from here and the next available bridge is several miles downriver.

10

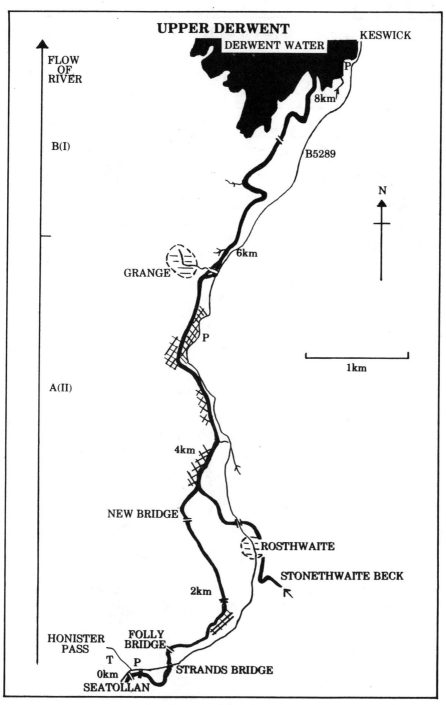

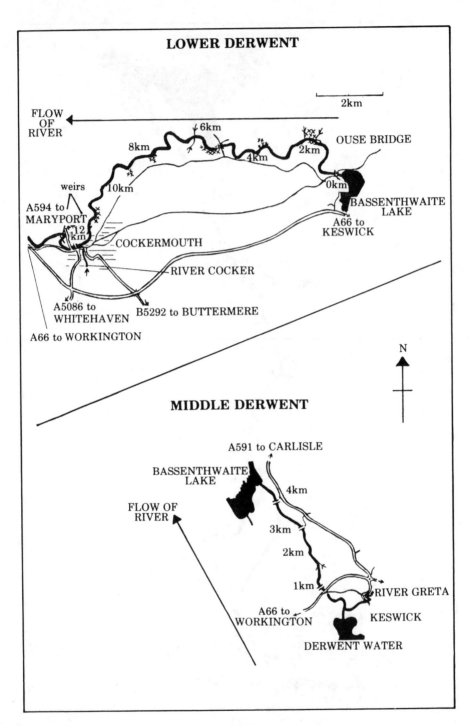

LOWER DERWENT

2km

FLOW
OF
RIVER

6km

OUSE BRIDGE

8km

2km

4km

2km

weirs 10km

0km

BASSENTHWAITE
LAKE

A594 to
MARYPORT

12
km

A66 to
KESWICK

COCKERMOUTH

RIVER COCKER

A5086 to
WHITEHAVEN

B5292 to BUTTERMERE

A66 to WORKINGTON

N

MIDDLE DERWENT

A591 to CARLISLE

BASSENTHWAITE
LAKE

4km

FLOW OF
RIVER

3km

2km

1km

RIVER GRETA

A66 to
WORKINGTON

KESWICK

DERWENT WATER

RIVER DUDDON

GRADE: III with sections of IV and V

TIME: 3 hours for the whole river

DETAILS:

	LENGTH	HEIGHT LOSS	GRADIENT
Upper	9km	100m	11m/km
Lower	6km	70m	11.7m/km

INDICATOR: The road bridge, Duddon bridge on the A595, G.R. 180.883, is supported on two pillars in the river. At the base of these pillars are concrete platforms. These need to be covered to make a trip worthwhile on the lower Duddon. The upper Duddon requires a few more inches of water to give a reasonable trip.

ACCESS:

Wrynose bottom (Cockley bridge)	256.017
Birks bridge	234.994
Cattle grid (500m south of Troutal)	234.983
Ulpha bridge	196.930
Bend in river (next to the road)	200.916
Duddon bridge	180.883

GENERAL DESCRIPTION

The river Duddon lies in the south Lake District. It drains the south central fells into a little-known estuary, which is a branch of Morecambe bay. There are two grade V sections, one in Wallowbarrow gorge, one behind Troutal farm. Most of the river has rapids of some sort, the valley itself being one of the least visited but most beautiful in the area.

The trips most often undertaken are from the cattle grid to Ulpha bridge, portaging the most difficult sections in Wallowbarrow gorge and after. From Ulpha bridge to Duddon bridge. Thus conveniently splitting the river into upper and lower sections.

DESCRIPTION

The upper sections of the river are shallow and require very heavy rain to make them canoeable. Apart from the fall (III), under Cockley bridge, the river is grade II until Birk's bridge is reached (and the map starts).

A(F)   Just above Birk's bridge the river narrows to about 1m, and loses about 4m in height. This is best avoided owing to the boulders hidden under the surface, under which the water flows.

B(III)   From the pool below the bridge, shallow rapids lead to an S-bend where the river leaves the road. After the S-bend things become a little harder.

C(V)   Troutal gorge. A 3m crag on the left signals the start of a series of small falls. A 20m crag on the right marks the grade V (possibly harder). Portage on the left bank. The water flows over, around and under huge boulders; the drop in height is lost in the size of the boulders. In spate this is an impressive sight.

13

D(III/IV)   More rapids follow, with a tricky part on a left bend. Then fast and continuous rapids, with many boulders to avoid, lead to a right bend, with the road on the left up a bank, where the cattle grid can be found. The gradient increases slightly and the river becomes more constricted in places, with few breakouts. Just upstream of where the trees on the right finish, a wire spans the river. This is used as a hand-rail for people using the stepping stones across the river. The river now widens slightly, the gradient eases and an S-bend with two islands follows.

E(III)   The first island is small with a few saplings on it; this is passed to the right if not covered. The second is larger and is passed on the left. A few bends follow presenting no great problem. On the right look out for a wall, fence and stile together: here Wallowbarrow gorge starts.

F(IV/V)   Wallowbarrow gorge. The gorge begins easy and gets progressively more difficult as you move downriver. A rapid by a 2m crag on the right is followed in 100m by a boulder 3.5m high and 5m wide. This acts as a log trap, as water flows underneath it – take care. A little further on an 8m-high monolith stands in the middle of the river. Land on the right and inspect. An awkward 1.5m drop is followed by 200m of difficult water, culminating in a 2m drop with no easy route. Portage on the right for most, especially if the river is not very high. Smaller falls lead in a few hundred metres to an arched footbridge at the end of the gorge.

G(II/III)   Now easier and a chance to relax. You will pass under Dunnerdale
(W)   bridge; after 1km a footbridge will be reached, with a weir. This has been done on the far left, but right is easier. Portage in high water (see plan). A pebbly island has formed below the weir. More easy water follows until an obvious drop in the river is reached.

H(III/IV)   The river flows through a very narrow gap at right-angles to the flow of the river; there is also a small drop and some awkward rocks to add to the difficulties. This is a tricky problem, and will unseat the less skilled paddler. This is followed by a boulder-strewn section, until the river drops more steeply over more boulders, with some very confused water, stoppers and standing waves, as the water is channelled through another narrow gap.
    After an almost flat stretch, an island is passed after a left bend. This is best taken to the left, down a steep rapid. Finally a succession of easier rapids lead to the bridge at Ulpha.

I(III)   Below the bridge the river is wider, and the rapids consist of standing waves, with the odd large stopper; between the rapids is calmer water. Before the road meets the river on the left side two islands must be negotiated. The first is covered in small trees and best taken to the left. The second island, a fair distance from the first, is again wooded, but much longer; the left side is obviously clear.
    After the road leaves the river there are some interesting rapids but none too difficult. Look out for two telegraph wires crossing the river high above. At this point is an island followed by a fall. This is best inspected.

J(IV)   Fortunately a bridge spans the river below the island. The island can be taken either side. The right side gives a better line into the fall. The fall should be taken on the right as a weir guards the left of the river. From the right side you will go down a steep incline, through a stopper

14

and end up on the left of the river beneath the bridge in a deep pool, admiring your skill if you make it.

K(W)   Two weirs follow in quick succession. The first is small, the second is much bigger with a good towback and closed at either end. This is best portaged.

L(III) Easier water leads shortly to the last rapid, which is quite long. The right side avoids the trees that stand on small islands in the river.

M(II) Flat water for the final kilometre brings you to Duddon bridge. On the left immediately downstream of the bridge a shallow slipway provides the easiest egress. A weir downriver of the bridge provides good sport for those who have not had enough.

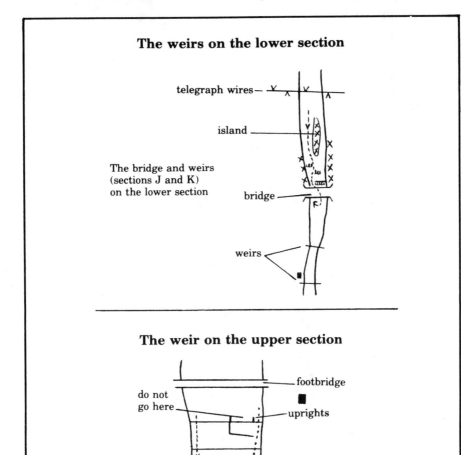

The weirs on the lower section

telegraph wires

island

The bridge and weirs
(sections J and K)
on the lower section

bridge

weirs

The weir on the upper section

footbridge

do not
go here

uprights

pebbly
island

15

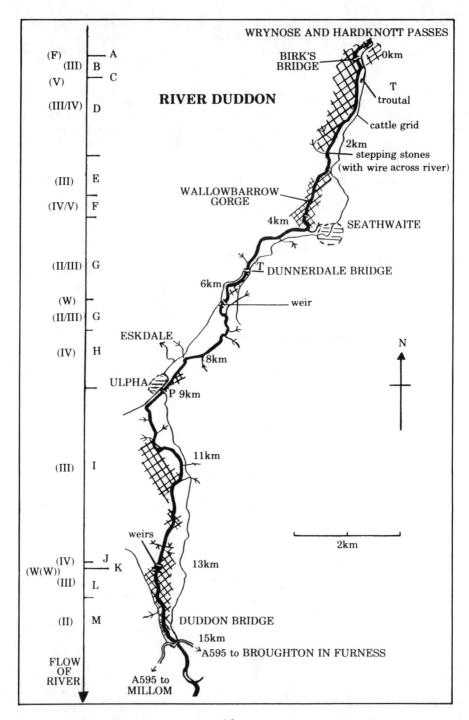

WRYNOSE AND HARDKNOTT PASSES

(F) A
(III) B
(V) C
(III/IV) D

RIVER DUDDON

BIRK'S
BRIDGE

0km

T
troutal

cattle grid

2km
stepping stones
(with wire across river)

(III) E
(IV/V) F

WALLOWBARROW
GORGE

4km

SEATHWAITE

(II/III) G

T DUNNERDALE BRIDGE

6km

(W)
(II/III) G

weir

ESKDALE

(IV) H

8km

N

ULPHA

P 9km

(III) I

11km

2km

weirs

(IV) J
(W(W)) K
(III) L

13km

(II) M

DUDDON BRIDGE

15km
A595 to BROUGHTON IN FURNESS

FLOW
OF
RIVER

A595 to
MILLOM

16

RIVER EAMONT

GRADE: I/II

TIME: 3 hours

DETAILS: LENGTH 18km   HEIGHT LOSS 60m   GRADIENT 3.3m/km

INDICATOR: The level of water flowing under the bridge at Pooley Bridge is shallow at normal summer levels.

ACCESS: Pooley Bridge   470.243
                  Eamont bridge   523.288
                  Brougham castle   538.291
                  Below this continue on to the Eden

GENERAL DESCRIPTION

The Eamont drains Ullswater, and flows east to join the river Eden below Penrith. At Brougham castle it is joined by the river Lowther. It is canoeable at most times of the year. It is more noted for its scenery than white water, the main excitement being provided by numerous weirs, all of which are shootable with care.

DESCRIPTION

(NB All grade II sections are I at low water levels)

A(II)   Starting on Ullswater, or at the bridge in Pooley Bridge, the river is flat.

B(W)   The first weir can be seen from above by two concrete uprights in the river.

C(II)   Dacre beck joins from the left after 1km. Half-way a footbridge will be found, followed by heavily wooded banks.

D(II)   The junction with the beck is followed by a bridge. Soon after this rougher water forms at the site of an old weir, the remains of which are easily visible on either bank.

E(I/II)   Easy water leads after 1.5km to an island.

F(W)   At the island the left channel is clear, the right channel holds a small weir.

G(II)   The river now flows in a large loop, passing under a footbridge. The railway viaduct is preceded by wooded islands which split the river into several channels. A smaller loop now follows, with wooded banks to another weir.

H(W)   This weir is easy angled and provides rough water. On the right bank soon after is a caravan site.

I(II)   More easy water leads to Eamont bridge. Egress on the left bank below the bridge.

J(W)   Soon after Eamont bridge, an awkward little weir is to be found. Both banks are lined with trees making inspection difficult.

K(I/II)   The river now flows across open fields; around a long left bend is another weir.

L(W)   This weir is sloping, and a stopper develops across the whole river.

M(I)	The A66 can be seen to the left.
N(W)	The final weir can be admired for its length. It lies at the confluence with the river Lowther, with Brougham castle guarding the whole scene.
O(I/II)	From here on the river meanders under some power lines. Past another loop in the river the banks become more wooded again. The river bends right under a cliff, and here an island may have blocked channels. This is followed by more cliffs with some caves. Finally the confluence with the river Eden is reached.

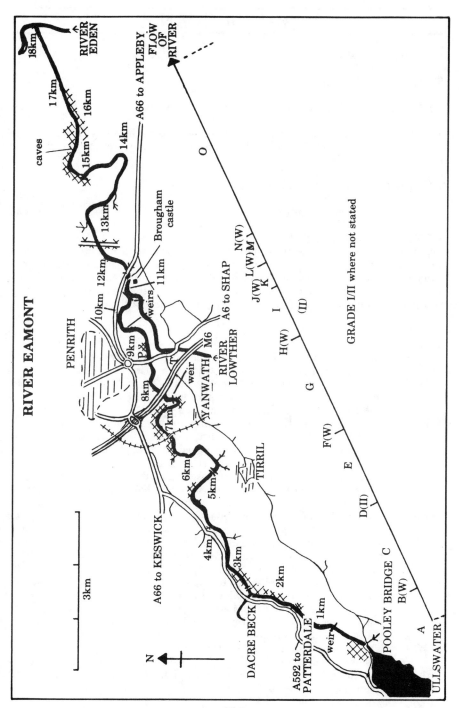

RIVER EAMONT

RIVER EDEN

GRADE: Mostly II with some parts of III

TIME: 2 hours

DETAILS: LENGTH 13km   HEIGHT LOSS 30m   GRADIENT 2.4m/km

INDICATOR: At low levels the water flows over Armathwaite weir only on the right of the river. All the rocks at the weir are covered when the river is in flood.

ACCESS: From the river Eamont
Lazonby   550.404
Armathwaite weir   503.453

GENERAL DESCRIPTION

The Eden is the site of a white water race, from Lazonby to Armathwaite. These two places offer the only access to the river. The river consists of flat sections interspersed by rapids, some of which are quite long, and in general they get harder as you progress down the river, though none of them is very difficult. It is possible to paddle the river from miles upriver but most of the river is reasonably flat.

DESCRIPTION

From the confluence with the river Eamont the Eden is mostly flat until a natural fall is reached after you pass under a railway bridge. This is Eden Lacy falls.

A(W)   This weir-type natural fall can be taken far right or to the left, but more awkward, of centre. At higher levels there are more possibilities but a large stopper forms in some places.

B(II)   Barely a grade II, the river winds its way past some caves in the sandstone cliffs on the right, until after 3km Lazonby is reached. At Lazonby a large layby provides a good starting place next to the river, upstream from the bridge. The river is at first flat, the first broken water consisting of standing waves which form over shingle banks. An S-bend starts with some broken rocks and has some broken water on the second bend.

C(II/III)   The rapids now are longer with more rocks in them, as the river passes into a beautiful and reasonably remote wooded valley, with some sandstone cliffs on either side of the river. One cliff should stand out as being higher than all the others on the left side of the river. This marks the site of a long grade III rapid, which flows mainly to the right of a shrubby shingle bank. The rapid after this has some large standing waves and a stopper which can be an excellent place to play at certain water levels. From here onwards the difficulties subside. Look out for some faces carved in the cliffs on the right bank. Eventually you will reach Armathwaite weir, which is semi-natural.

D(W)   This is most often taken on the right, though the left is somewhat easier at some water levels. (In any case the access agreement requires you to egress above the weir on the left bank by a stone shed, and follow signs to the road.)

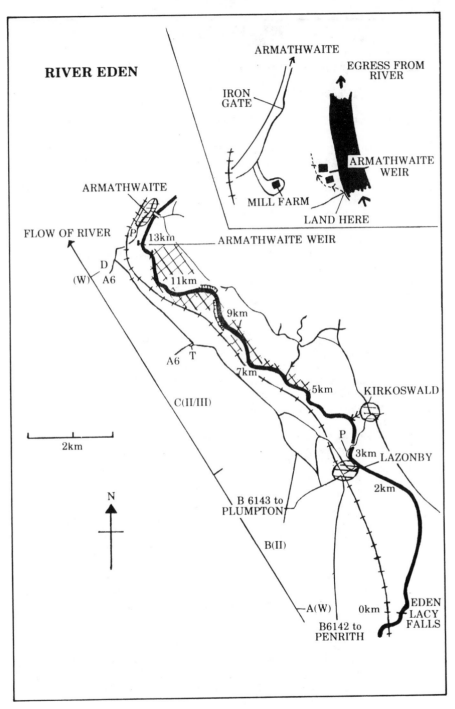

RIVER EDEN

ARMATHWAITE

EGRESS FROM
RIVER

IRON
GATE

ARMATHWAITE
WEIR

MILL FARM

LAND HERE

ARMATHWAITE

FLOW OF RIVER

ARMATHWAITE WEIR

P 13km

D

(W)   A6

11km

9km

A6   T

7km

5km   KIRKOSWALD

C(II/III)

2km

P

3km LAZONBY

2km

N

B 6143 to
PLUMPTON

B(II)

A(W)   0km   EDEN
LACY
FALLS

B6142 to
PENRITH

21

RIVER ESK

GRADE: II with several sections of III

TIME: 1½ hours

DETAILS: LENGTH 8km   HEIGHT LOSS 85m GRADIENT 10.07m/km

INDICATOR: If there is adequate water flowing over the shingle below the bridge at the end of the trip the river will be high enough.

ACCESS: Brotherikeld farm   212.013
                  The bridge at G.R.   149.995
                  Access at other places is possible but not easy.

GENERAL DESCRIPTION

The Esk flows down Eskdale to the sea at Ravenglass. Most of the river is lined by trees, and low branches can be a problem. Although only grade II, the river can only be paddled after heavy rain. This means that although the river is not difficult, the flow is fast and quite powerful.

DESCRIPTION

A(II)   From Brotherikeld farm the flow is swift. After only 200m the difficulties increase, and a large tree branch lies in the river. After this, which lies on a long bend, the flow eases to the point where the river becomes shallow as you near the road. No further problems are likely to be encountered until you reach Doctor's bridge.

B(III)   Just above Doctor's bridge the water is slightly more difficult. The route is obvious, between two large stoppers.

C(II)   Easier again; trees line the banks.

D(III)   The river disappears around a right bend into a gorge. Standing waves and some small folding waves form here. With a less experienced group this is best inspected. The gorge is about 100m long and finishes under a bridge consisting of two 30cm-wide girders. After the gorge boulders provide some interesting water.

E(II/III) Again easier water flows between many overhanging trees. After 1km an island is reached. The middle channel is best followed. The right channel should be avoided, as it flows through many trees before joining the river again.

          This is soon followed by a bridge, and 100m below this, large boulders form confused water and stoppers. Now easier again until a right bend is reached. On this bend a large slab of rock divides the river. The right side provides an easy chicken run. The left side is more restricted and large standing waves, followed by small stoppers, form. The slab provides a useful eddy, from which you can play on the waves. At certain heights of the river it is possible to get popouts. The last kilometre-and-a-half is easier, passing under a footbridge half-way. There is a large layby, by the bridge at the finish of the trip. Below this the water is mostly grade I to the sea.

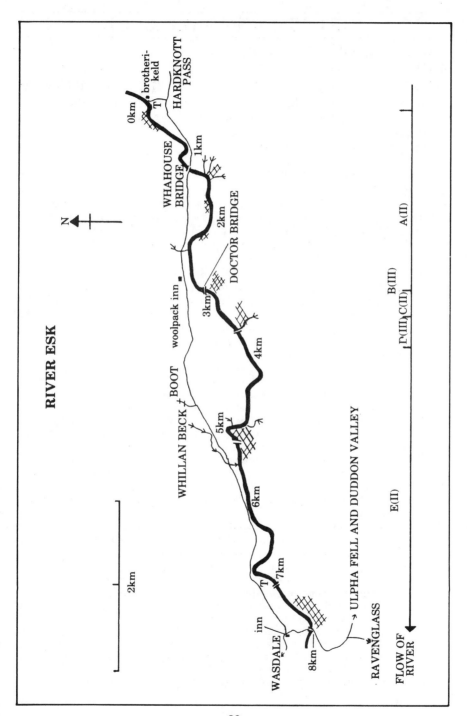

RIVER ESK

N

2km

HARDKNOTT PASS

brotheri-keld

T

0km

WHAHOUSE BRIDGE

1km

DOCTOR BRIDGE

2km

woolpack inn

3km

4km

BOOT

WHILLAN BECK

5km

6km

T

7km

inn

WASDALE

8km

RAVENGLASS

→ ULPHA FELL AND DUDDON VALLEY

A(II)

B(III)

C(II)

D(III)

E(II)

FLOW OF RIVER

GREAT LANGDALE BECK

GRADE: II then III then IV then II

TIME: 2 hours

DETAILS: LENGTH 6km   HEIGHT LOSS 37m   GRADIENT 6m/km

INDICATOR: If you can get on the water at the bridge at the Old Dungeon Ghyll hotel the river will be worth a paddle.

ACCESS:
Old Dungeon Ghyll hotel bridge	285.060
Baysbrown bridge	317.053
Weir at Chapel Stile	325.053
Elterwater bridge	327.047

GENERAL DESCRIPTION

Great Langdale beck flows from the head of the Langdale valley to Elterwater. The first section is easy though fast flowing as some stretches have been canalized to prevent flooding. The rapids proper start after 3.5km. The upper section is worth doing for the scenery alone. After the weir in Chapel Stile the most difficult section leads to Elterwater bridge.

DESCRIPTION

A(II)   Park at the Old Dungeon Ghyll car park. Start the river at the bridge you have just crossed, on the downstream side. The flow is swift, but the water easy, and eddies are rare. After you pass under the B5343 bridge, and the bridge next to it, several steps will be encountered; these hold standing waves on which to play. The river continues at a similar grade until a bridge, followed by a pool with woodland on the right bank, is reached. This is Baysbrown bridge.

B(III)   The river bends right and left. Many rocks will trap the unwary. At the end of the long straight is a left-right tight S-bend. This can be rather tricky. At the bottom is a stopper which will give good sport. Slightly easier, a left bend sees the start of a long series of standing waves which bring you to a footbridge, and a large boulder, before the flat top section of the weir at Chapel Stile.

C(W)   The weir is a large sloping one, and can be taken safely almost anywhere. The left side is rather shallow, at the bottom of the weir.

D(III)   You may choose to inspect the next section from below the weir or paddle around the right-hand bend and quickly gain a breakout on the right.

E(IV)   This is Pillar falls and should be inspected. This is the site where a canoeist was stuck in his canoe in the middle of the river for 45 minutes while the river was in full flood. The front end of his boat was trapped under jagged rocks, which face upstream in the middle of this fall. It is best to take this fall on the far right, clipping the guarding boulder as close as possible. Portage on the right is easy.

F(III)   It is possible to get in immediately below the falls down a steep bank. The next section is a steep grade III, usually taken towards the left side near the high slate walls of the Pillar time-share complex. The next fall is big but safe, the stopper at the bottom tending to throw you one way or the other. Easier, if fast water leads to the bridge at Elterwater. Egress below the bridge on the left.

G(II)   Calmer water eventually brings you without further difficulty to Elter water (lake).

24

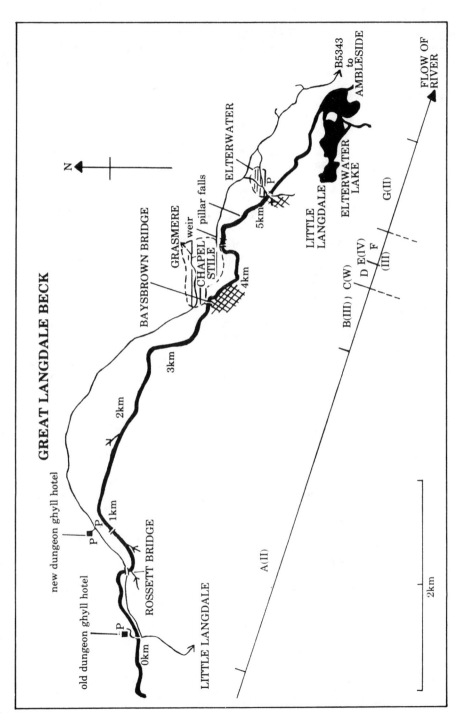

RIVER GRETA

GRADE: II–III

TIME: 2 hours

DETAILS: LENGTH 8km   HEIGHT LOSS 60m   GRADIENT 7.5m/km

INDICATOR: From the road into Keswick from the east, the island in section J can be seen, if you can pass the island the river will be canoeable.

ACCESS:

Bridge on the river Glendaramackin	319.248
Confluence of the Glendaramackin with St Johns beck	315.247
A small park in Keswick	277.239
Bridge in Keswick	264.237

GENERAL DESCRIPTION

The Greta, despite its shallow overall gradient, provides a good trip. Away from the road for most of its length, but followed by the course of a disused railway, the river gives you a feeling of isolation for the first half of the journey. Many parts are easy, but the rapids can be tricky. In spate conditions it provides an excellent and sustained ride. The Greta flows from St Johns-in-the-Vale to join the river Derwent just below Keswick.

DESCRIPTION

A(II) Starting on the Glendaramackin in a fairly swift flow around a series of bends will bring you to a road bridge and the confluence with St Johns beck.

B(II) The first section is wide and slow flowing, leading under a railway bridge, to some large boulders in the river. Smaller rocks follow to another railway bridge. A right bend leads to a steeper shallower stretch underneath another railway bridge.

C(III) A corrugated hut on the right bank indicates the magnetic rock rapid. The top of this rapid is straightforward, but at the bottom most of the water flows at a large smooth rock, often just covered. This catches many people unaware.

D(II) Downstream is again easier, to another long, shallow rapid. More rocks and a steeper gradient lead to yet another railway bridge.

E(III) Soon a long rapid is reached. This is the best section on the river. Many rocks confine the flow of the river. Several routes are viable, stoppers form in high water and many breakouts are to be found. A sharp bend at the bottom with a small stopper on the left and an eddy opposite finish the section. Easier water follows to an eddy on the right before the river bends left.

F(II) Around the corner is an island. Taken either side, and followed by a rock-strewn section, another railway bridge is reached, followed by a broken weir.

26

G(III)(W) Several metal bolts 20cm high protrude from the concrete. A safe passage is easily found. Many boulders provide confused water, and another railway bridge follows.

H(II) Now easier water flows past a large island; the right channel is so small you may well miss it. A caravan site is on the left bank.

I(III)(W) Just past the caravan site is another broken weir. At low levels a sneaky route behind a 1m boulder is best. At higher levels the right side is best. Half-way down this rapid a rock shelf lies under the water; this constricts the main flow to the right bank. Negotiating this can be quite tricky at certain levels.

J(II–III) Standing waves follow, then easier water to the dual carriageway high above. A small arched bridge lies above a shelf in the river bed, where a playful stopper forms on the right. Small rapids come in quick succession, until a 3m boulder on the left is reached. Now rock shelves cause rapids to be formed, the middle being the best route. Two more bridges are followed by an island, which has hanging trees over the more favourable right-hand channel.

K(II) A shallow rapid precedes a footbridge. Then a road bridge, another shallow rapid and another footbridge.

L(II) Another shallow rapid leads directly to a small weir which should cause no problems. Flatter water follows. A sweeping bend to the left and a wall on the right lead to the road bridge.

M(I–II) After the road bridge a ramp on the right provides the best egress. On downstream easy water leads to the river Derwent.

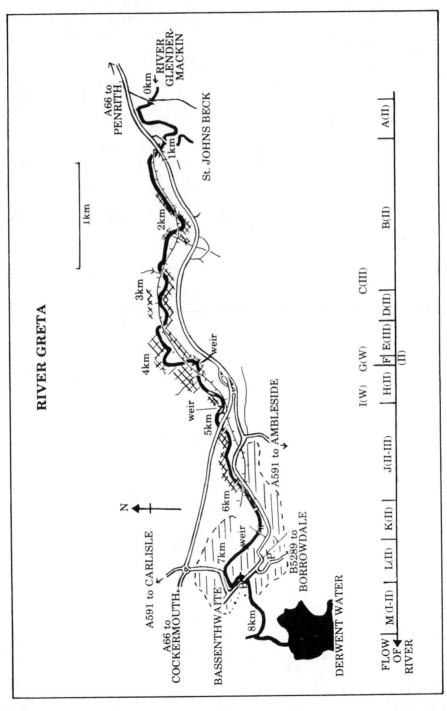

RIVER KENT

GRADE: Upper II/III   Lower II/IV

TIME: Upper   2½ hours   Lower   1 hour

DETAILS:

	LENGTH	HEIGHT LOSS	GRADIENT
Upper	14km	65m	4.6m/km
Lower	4.5km	30m	6.6m/km

INDICATOR: Upper   In the village of Staveley when in flood the river is only a few inches below the level of the opposite bank. If you can float down this section then the river will be paddleable.

               Lower   The lower Kent is paddleable at most times of the year. Looking upriver from Sedgwick bridge, at low levels the water flows down a narrow gorge, at higher levels the water flows over the sandstone slabs on the left (as you look at it) before dropping into the main flow.

ACCESS: Upper

Bridge to Kentmere (and downriver for 1km)	467.995
Staveley	473.978
Bowston	498.966
Burneside	506.955
Kendal	517.918

               Lower

Scrogg's weir	513.906
Prizet bridge	512.892
Sedgwick bridge	507.868
Sandside (in the estuary if the tide is in)	478.807

NB It is possible to get out below Force falls but the land is private (see the section on access)   507.865

GENERAL DESCRIPTION

The Kent flows from Kentmere reservoir to the estuary at Arnside, where a tidal bore forms on spring tides. The stretch in the Kentmere valley is narrow and possibly never paddled, though it is not so very difficult, and requires a lot of rain. The usual trip on the upper part of the river starts at the bridge at the bottom of the Kentmere valley just outside Staveley. There is a difficult fall here. The upper section is not difficult apart from the many weirs and a rapid under a factory. Scrogg's weir south of Kendal marks the end of the upper section. Below this the river flows through several narrow gorges some of which have undercut rock walls. The last 400m is excellent and includes two big falls.

DESCRIPTION

A(IV)   Starting above the bridge the river is split by large areas of rock. The right side is deepest and includes a 1.5m drop; the left side flows down angled slabs. After the bridge is a rocky fall with several possibilities depending on the water level.

B(II)   Easy water leads to a flat pool above a weir.

C(W)	This is a 3m steeply angled weir. You can expect to bounce a bit if you decide to do it. Under a bridge, and then another weir, newly constructed, will be found. Vertical concrete pillars split the flow. It is not known how safe this weir is.
D(II)	The water flows swiftly through the village of Staveley. The river Gowan (a beck) increases the flow of the river in the village. The river leaves the road and flows off across the fields. The rapids are mostly small but some have overhanging bushes.
E(III)	On seeing a bridge take care – a wire spans the river. Not far down the river the water disappears under a factory. This is guarded by a complicated weir, and the water under the factory is III+, but difficult to inspect. This section is not easy but has been paddled.
F(II)	Almost flat water brings you to the village of Bowston. The river seems to disappear.
G(W)	In fact there is a 3m+ weir, with shallow landings. This weir should be portaged.
H(II)	More easy water leads under Bowston bridge and on to another weir.
I(W)	This weir has recently been renovated and new fish steps added. It is not known how safe all parts of this weir are.
J(II)	Below the weir a few tight twists and more easier water lead you to the village of Burneside. The river disappears between high brick walls round a corner, and under a long bridge. This should present no problems. Now swifter, the river is joined by the Sprint, flows under a footbridge and is joined by the Mint before entering a large pool with life rings on the banks. On leaving the pool you enter the town of Kendal.
(W)	Under a railway bridge and then a road bridge, and stop. A 2m weir which can be nasty in high water. After this all the way through the town the banks are canalized. Many small waves and stoppers form on man-made shelves. Eventually you pass under another road bridge, where you can get out on the right if the river is low. After the houses are passed, the river becomes more sluggish until Scrogg's weir is reached. It is possible to get out on the right above the weir.
K(W)	The weir is shallow angled and usually a scrape.
L(II)	Easy water leads after some distance to Prizet bridge, where the flow becomes swifter.
M(III)	A sloping drop of about 2m into a gorge with undercut rocks gives some large standing waves. More rapids lead to a long steep section with a cliff on the left bank. At the top a few spikes mark the location of an old weir. The rapid is quite long and has some big stoppers through which you must go. This is followed by more small rapids. On reaching an island the left side is best. Easy water leads to a footbridge above a weir.
N(W)	Flat water leads to a weir. This is one of the area's notorious spots. Many people each year lose their canoes, paddles and in some cases nearly their lives in this weir. The tow back is strong and the apparent tongue in the middle is not as good as it looks. To add to this the left bank is someone's garden, and quite understandably the owner is anti-canoeing because of people portaging across his lawn. He has been known to lock boats in his garage. Portage on the right bank.
O(III)	On seeing Sedgwick bridge you will another rapid similar to the one at Prizet bridge. Make sure you can get out just under the road bridge on the left, before you do this rapid.

P(IV+)   Directly after the bridge is a 1.5m vertical drop. The stopper will easily hold a boat and in flood exceeds the height of the fall itself. At low levels this can be taken in a number of places. Portage on the left if you are not sure. This fall has also eaten many boats and given their occupants heart-stopping moments.

Q(W)
R(IV)   Easier water now leads to an island, a new sloping weir has been built across the river at the top of the island.
After this island its Force falls, a 3m+ fall. It is normally taken on the left under the end of some twigs of a branch which overhangs the left bank. The speed you gain on the fall bursts you through the stopper if the river is not too high. Several boats have been damaged here. After your heart rate returns to normal, egress on the right bank up a slipway just after the dual carriageway bridge.

S(II)   The remainder of the river is flat and leads to the Kent estuary after about 5km. A specific request has been made to avoid continuing through Levens Park estate.

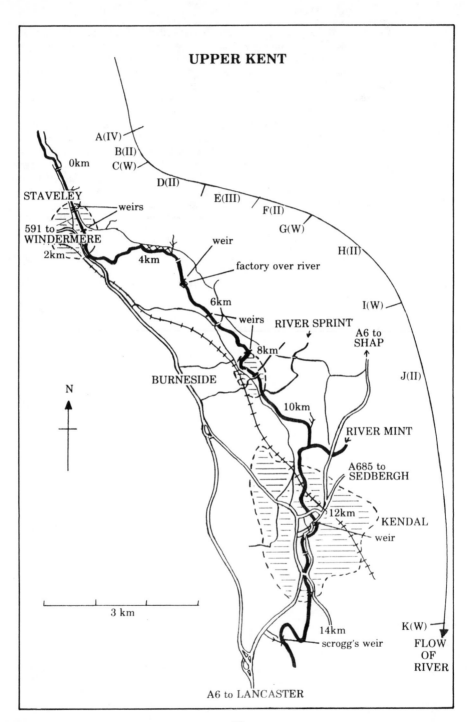

UPPER KENT

A(IV)
B(II)
0km
C(W)

STAVELEY

weirs

D(II)

E(III)

F(II)

G(W)

591 to
WINDERMERE

2km

4km

weir

H(II)

factory over river

6km

I(W)

weirs

RIVER SPRINT

8km

A6 to
SHAP

N

BURNESIDE

J(II)

10km

RIVER MINT

A685 to
SEDBERGH

12km

KENDAL

weir

3 km

14km
scrogg's weir

K(W)

FLOW
OF
RIVER

A6 to LANCASTER

32

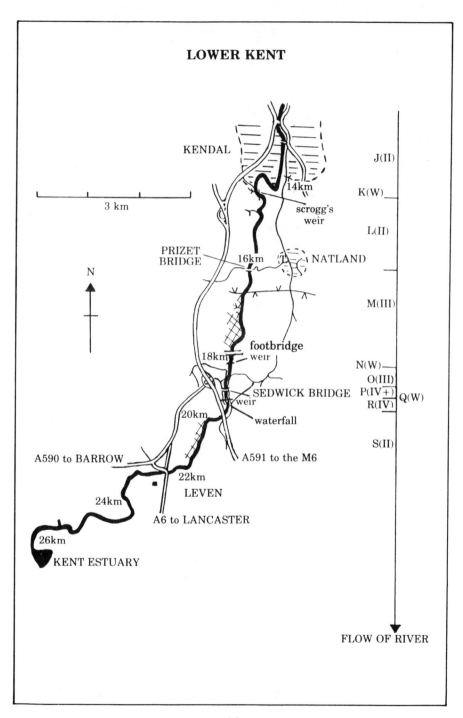

LOWER KENT

KENDAL

14km

scrogg's weir

3 km

J(II)

K(W)

L(II)

PRIZET BRIDGE   16km   T   NATLAND

N

M(III)

footbridge

18km   weir

N(W)

O(III)

P(IV+)

Q(W)

R(IV)

SEDWICK BRIDGE

weir

20km   waterfall

S(II)

A590 to BARROW

A591 to the M6

22km

LEVEN

24km

A6 to LANCASTER

26km

KENT ESTUARY

FLOW OF RIVER

RIVER LEVEN

GRADE: III

TIME: 15 mins to the end of the race course
50 mins to Haverthwaite bridge

DETAILS: LENGTH 3.5km   HEIGHT LOSS 42m   GRADIENT 10.5m/km

INDICATOR: See notes on ACCESS

ACCESS:

B road 100m from the bridge at Newby bridge	368.864
Field on left of the river	356.855
Backbarrow bridge, right bank	355.852
A590 road bridge	354.843
Haverthwaite bridge	345.836

GENERAL DESCRIPTION
The Leven drains Windermere into Morecambe bay. The fall at Backbarrow bridge has been the site of many dramas. Below is an unshootable weir, followed by a large stopper across the river. NB The river is open to canoeists *only on certain days*, arranged each year by Lakeland Canoe Club.

DESCRIPTION
A(III) The bridge at Newby bridge is where the river proper starts. Above this the river is wide and more like an extension to the lake. Downstream from the bridge is a small weir. Next to the right bank below this weir is the B road where you normally start the river. At the weir some water is diverted down a side channel, which has flood gates; these are only open when the river is high. From the weir the flood channel rejoins after about 100m. Then follows a series of rapids.

(W) The brickchute, normally taken in the middle between the concrete uprights.
Mill force, a 2m drop with a large stopper to the left of a rocky island. The chicken run on the right of the island has a small stopper at the bottom.
A flatter section, leading to a 1m drop, again with a playful stopper on the right side.
A series of standing waves across the river.
A long rocky rapid with a considerable drop from top to bottom. The right side is much rockier.
Another 2m drop, with large standing waves on the right.
A long rock-strewn section with several small stoppers at the bottom. Normally you should egress on the left at the edge of the field.

B(W) Downstream is a 2.5m weir which has a rocky landing, but may be negotiated in several places.

C(F) The fall at Backbarrow bridge should be inspected. The fall itself lies under the arched bridge, to add to the difficulties. A flat pool provides an opportunity to pick up the pieces. This fall has been successfully done on many occasions, but has also wrecked many boats.

34

D(W)	At the other end of the flat pool is a weir. PORTAGE. A 1m drop on to sharp rocks, followed by a steep series of gobbling stoppers, is best avoided. An attempt on this resulted in a written-off boat and, according to the story, almost the paddler as well.
E(W)	30m after this another fall/weir has another large stopper.
F(III)	Standing waves lead to a low footbridge, after which is an island. The top of the island lies level with a small weir. As you pass the island the waves grow in size to produce probably the largest standing waves in the county under the A590 road bridge. Egress on the right if you are to finish here.
G(W)	400m downstream is a shootable 3.5m weir (angled). Avoid the fish steps on the right of the river.
H(III)	A short easy section leads to another island. A footbridge, now damaged, once spanned the river at this island. The right side has been done, but contains metal stakes and bars as well as a bouncy rapid. The left side is steep, with large waves, depositing most through the stopper at its end. After all the excitement it is possible to paddle between the trees to regain the right channel again and take two more weirs, both of which have playful(?) stoppers. It is easier to continue down the left channel.
I(II)	After the channels rejoin, another island, heavily wooded, can be passed on either side without problem, before the bridge at Haverthwaite is reached.

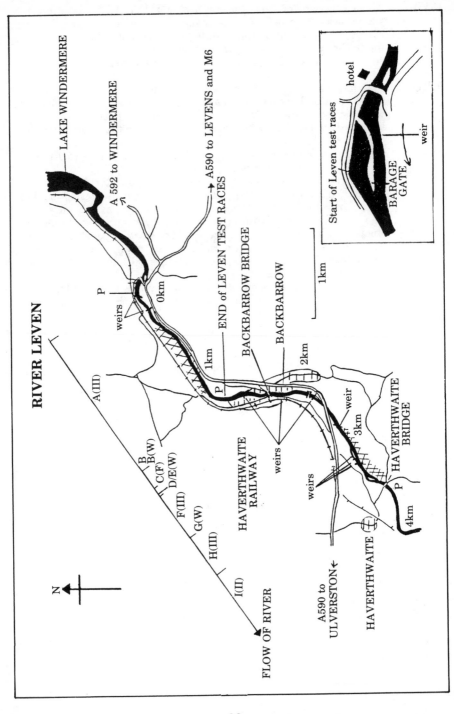

RIVER LEVEN

LAKE WINDERMERE

A 592 to WINDERMERE

A590 to LEVENS and M6

END of LEVEN TEST RACES

BACKBARROW BRIDGE

BACKBARROW

1km

P

weirs

0km

P

1km

P

2km

weir

3km

4km

P

HAVERTHWAITE BRIDGE

HAVERTHWAITE RAILWAY

weirs

weirs

A(III)

B
B(W)
C(F)
D/E(W)
F(III)
G(W)
H(III)
I(II)

N

FLOW OF RIVER

A590 to ULVERSTON

HAVERTHWAITE

Start of Leven test races

hotel

weir

BARAGE GATE

RIVER LOWTHER

GRADE: II with several short sections of III in high water. No portages

TIME: About 2 hours

DETAILS: LENGTH 5.5km HEIGHT LOSS 41m GRADIENT 7.7m/km

INDICATOR: If the weir just below Askham bridge is navigable then the river is also.

ACCESS:	Askam bridge	518.328
	Lowther bridge	525.282
	Brougham castle	538.291

The owner of the Lowther estates has requested that he should be contacted before a trip is undertaken. Contact L.A.O. for details.

GENERAL DESCRIPTION

The river Lowther flows from Wet Sleddale reservoir to its confluence with the river Eamont just below Penrith. Its watershed includes a great part of the Shap fells, and Haweswater reservoir. The first kilometre-and-a-half below the reservoir drops over 30m and would be paddleable in flood, at grade II–IV+, but low branches and narrow banks would cause problems. Below this much of the river is flat and slow flowing. The stretch from Askham bridge to Eamont bridge is of more interest, the rapids being generally easy and strewn with boulders.

DESCRIPTION

A	Park on the west side of the river and carry your canoes 50m along a track to a large pool above a weir.
B(W)	The weir is easy angled, and the only real difficulties lie in avoiding the small trees growing out of the weir. At low levels the left side is best.
C(II)	An easy but long rapid strewn with rocks gives the flavour of what is to follow.
D(II)	A left bend with larger waves is indicated by small cliffs directly ahead.
E(II)	Pass the island to the left following any route that is deep enough.
F(W)	Here a bridge is immediately followed by a small vertical weir, with a concrete sill above. This makes it difficult to pick up much speed.
G(II+)	This rapid is the first on the river where most of the water is channelled into the same route.
H(II)	Easier running rapids with many boulders lead past a caravan site on the left. As a sharp left bend approaches slow down and choose your line past an island.
I(III)	At low levels a shingle bank on the left will bar your route, forcing you right. You will then need to cut through between this and a small wall (see plan). The right-hand route around the island has nothing to offer. 50m downstream a small natural shelf can be taken almost anywhere.
J(III)	Around the next bend a short, steep rapid will require some skill to negotiate without problem.
K(II)	This island can be most easily negotiated via the far right channel, but at high levels low branches make the left route more viable.

L(II)   The supporting pillar of the Hugh's crag railway viaduct splits the river in two. The left channel, although deeper, *must* be avoided, as the bottom end holds a net of trees and bushes. The right channel is straightforward.

M(I–II)   The river now slows, and several large trees lie in the river. Also you will pass underneath the M6.

N(I)   Egress on the right bank upstream of the bridge, or continue on flat water to the confluence with the Eamont a further kilometre-and-a-half downriver.

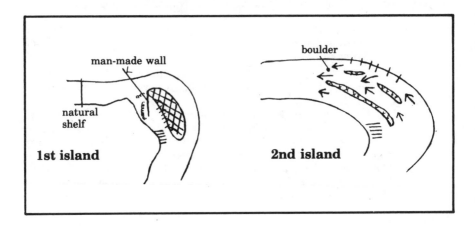

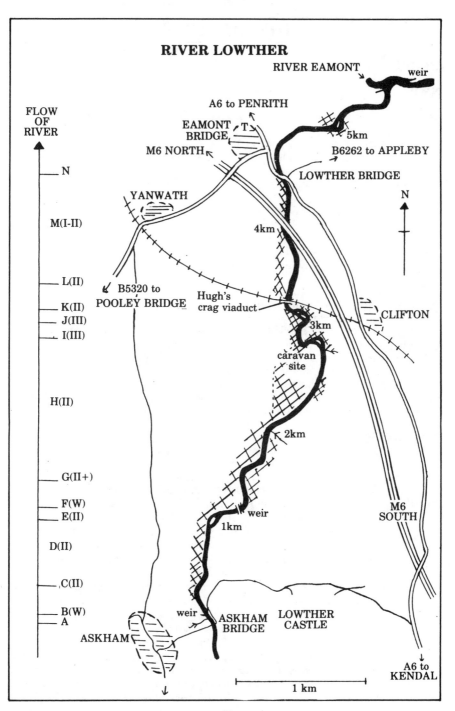

RIVER LOWTHER

RIVER EAMONT

weir

FLOW
OF
RIVER

A6 to PENRITH

EAMONT
BRIDGE

T

5km

N

M6 NORTH

B6262 to APPLEBY

LOWTHER BRIDGE

N

YANWATH

M(I-II)

4km

L(II)

B5320 to
POOLEY BRIDGE

Hugh's
crag viaduct

K(II)

J(III)

CLIFTON

I(III)

3km

caravan
site

H(II)

2km

G(II+)

F(W)

M6
SOUTH

E(II)

weir

D(II)

1km

C(II)

B(W)

weir

A

ASKHAM
BRIDGE

LOWTHER
CASTLE

ASKHAM

A6 to
KENDAL

1 km

RIVER LUNE

GRADE: III

TIME: 2½ hours

DETAILS: LENGTH 14km   HEIGHT LOSS 70m   GRADIENT 5m/km

INDICATOR: At the Crook of Lune bridge there is an island. The river is at its easiest when low; at this island you will scrape rocks as you pass it at low levels.

ACCESS:		
	Tebay bridge	613.028
	Crook of Lune Bridge	620.963
	Lincolns Inn bridge	632.923
	Killington New bridge	622.908
	Rawthey confluence	628.896
	Rigmaden bridge	616.848
	Devil's bridge (Kirby Lonsdale)	616.783

GENERAL DESCRIPTION

The Lune originates as many small rivers to the north of the Howgill fells. When they come together the river is flat for many miles until it reaches Tebay. Here is a difficult fall (IV), under an old bridge after this is easier until the Crook of Lune bridge is reached. From here a variety of rapids come at regular intervals until Killington New bridge. From here there are two weirs followed by more rapids. After the confluence with the Rawthey the river is grade I/II to Kirby Lonsdale, where the last half-mile is probably III. From here to the estuary at Lancaster flat water meanders across open fields, the only excitement being several weirs and a grade III rapid at Halton where slaloms are held.

DESCRIPTION

A(IV)   About half a mile south of the village of Tebay the A685 passes over the Lune. There is an old bridge, and immediately upstream of this bridge is a difficult rapid and fall. Around the corner are a few tricky rapids, but as you pass under the A road bridge the river gets easier.

B(II/III)   There are no really difficult rapids until the Crook of Lune bridge, except for an island just after a small bridge which can produce a heavy rapid under certain conditions. At the Crook of Lune bridge is a small island with a shallow rapid on either side. Around the bend the water quickens as the river narrows. After a few hundred metres another island can be taken easily through standing waves on the left, or with more difficulty on the right. A flatter stretch now leads to another island with a shallow rapid on either side. The river becomes more restricted now and on a slight left bend is a long rapid.

C(III)   The river at normal levels flows down a channel 6–7m wide; this produces some large waves, but there are no rocks to cause problems. The rapid is nearly 100m long, but has good breakouts at the bottom. A footbridge crosses the river, and the water becomes easier but swirly. A pleasant chute is soon reached, and then another narrow section, again quite long but more difficult than the last narrows. There is a reasonable drop in the river level here, and several stoppers must be negotiated as well as the standing waves. More swirly water and small rapids eventually bring you to the old railway viaduct.

D(II)   Now easier, the rapids are shallower and the river wider. When you see a lot of small trees and grass on the right and many rocks and small channels, care should be taken.

E(III/IV)   A series of standing waves lead to a series of stoppers which is followed by a slot only 2m wide, between a large boulder and a rocky reef. The slot also drops about 1.5m.

F(III)   From here Lincoln's Inn bridge is only 100m (in fact this can be seen from the top of the last rapid). Below the bridge is a rapid with big standing waves. The river turns left and a big bouncy rapid is soon followed by another slot which should be inspected.

G(IV)   Another reef spans the river but is broken on the right of middle but is only 2.5m wide. To add to the difficulties the river drops a few metres in a short distance, and the narrow part bends slightly and has several boulders in it which form stoppers. Many people have had to roll at the end of this rapid. A portage on the left side is easy.

H(III)   More swirly water and pleasant rapids follow, the last one being the most difficult. Here the water after the rapid is forced to the left by a rocky outcrop. There are many rocks confusing the water. After this is Killington New bridge.

I(W)   Downstream from the bridge is a weir; this can be taken towards the right on a vague chute, but has a big towback. If the water is at all high it is best portaged.

J(III)   A series of interesting and playful rapids bring you to flat water above a weir.

K(W)   This is Stangerthwaite weir. This weir has seen more dramas than the rest of the river. The stopper has a huge towback and is very powerful in high water.

L(III)   Below the weir is the Div 2 slalom site. Several man-made/natural obstructions produce some big standing waves. Again easy water leads to a shingle bank on the right, with a shallow rapid. At the bottom the river bends left into a small wooded gorge, which holds many standing waves. As the gorge fades a final series of standing waves leads to the confluence with the river Rawthey. It is normal to paddle around the next bend and get out on the left near the edge of the woods.

From here to Kirkby Lonsdale and Caton is mainly easy water with only a few small rapids.

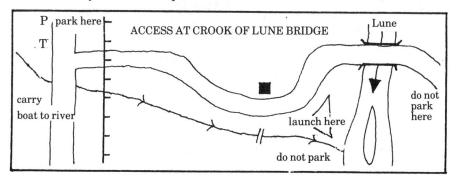

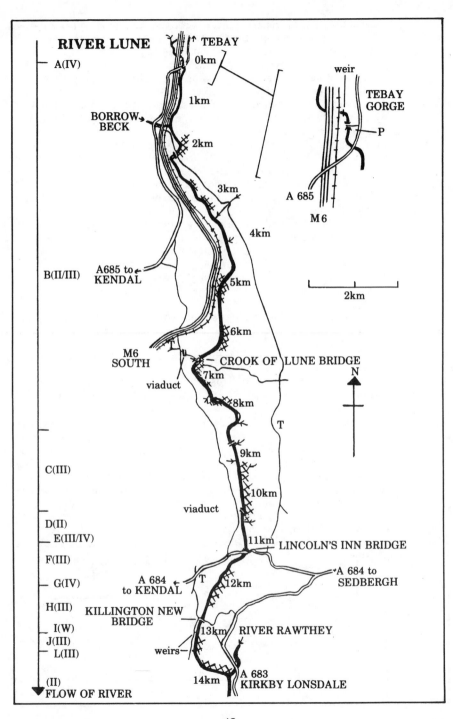

RIVER LUNE
A(IV)

TEBAY
0km

1km

BORROW
BECK

2km

3km

4km

A685 to
KENDAL

B(II/III)

5km

6km

M6
SOUTH

CROOK OF LUNE BRIDGE

7km

viaduct

8km

9km

C(III)

10km

viaduct

D(II)
E(III/IV)

11km   LINCOLN'S INN BRIDGE

F(III)

G(IV)

A 684
to KENDAL

A 684 to
SEDBERGH

12km

H(III)

KILLINGTON NEW
BRIDGE

I(W)
J(III)
L(III)

13km   RIVER RAWTHEY

weirs

(II)
FLOW OF RIVER

14km

A 683
KIRKBY LONSDALE

weir

TEBAY
GORGE

P

A 685

M 6

2km

N

RIVER MINT

GRADE: III with two short sections of IV

TIME: 3 hours for the full trip

DETAILS: LENGTH 12km   HEIGHT LOSS 143mGRADIENT 12.25m/km

INDICATOR: If it is possible to canoe under the Laverock bridge, the river will be worth doing.

ACCESS: From the A6 down a steep wooded bank

(Bannisdale low bridge)	543.011
Rossill bridge	554.996
Patton bridge (and the road 300m to the north)	557.974
Laverock bridge (and the road for 200m either way on the north side of the river)	536.952
Mint bridge (north side, downstream end)	522.943

GENERAL DESCRIPTION

The Mint flows from Bannisdale to join the Kent just above Burneside. Steep and small to start, it soon grows in size after 1km when Ashstead beck flows into it from the left. Generally grade II, with the rapid sections all being graded III and different in nature. In high flood low trees cause problems in several places and large standing waves develop. It is normally canoeable after heavy rain, or otherwise from Patton bridge only.

DESCRIPTION

A(II)   200m north of Bannisdale low bridge a minor road has a large layby. Park here, and carry to the bridge. At the bridge a steep slope leads down to the river. Under the bridge is a 2.5m drop, but the slot at the top is too narrow for a kayak. Immediately after this trees usually block the river. From this tree 80m of grade II lead to an eddy on the left at a right bend. Egress here, for just below nasty rocks guard a 10m fall.

B(IV)   Immediately below the fall, a narrow and twisty gorge can be found. This is easily portaged. The gorge ends in a mesh fence which could cause problems in flood conditions.

C(III)   50m after the first fence is a second fence. These will both be portaged. After the second fence is a small island. Get back on here. Either side of the island is shallow. So far a scrappy start, but from here the situation improves.

A 0.5m drop leads to a 2m fall followed by a steep section, of a series of small drops and continuous rapids. At one point, after the difficulties ease, a bush covers the right side of the river. The river now gets easier, until a footbridge is reached.

D(II–III)   Soon after the bridge, a single strand of wire spans the river at an awkward height. More easy rapids follow until the confluence with Ashstead beck is reached. At this confluence another fence blocks the river and care is needed.

43

E(II)	From the confluence low trees can be a problem for about 200m. On reaching a wall on the left the flow quickens but trees are less of a problem.
F(II)	Rossill bridge can be recognized by its conspicuous white railings. This is immediately followed by a second bridge. Both banks are lined by trees. On a slight left bend a bough hangs in the river. At reasonable levels it is possible to canoe over this, at lower levels a portage may be necessary. 300m downstream a sharp right bend is found. On this bend a wooden fence hangs into the river. It may be possible to sneak past the fence on the left. But be prepared to portage again. After this the banks have been reinforced in many places, and the river is calmer. Passing under two bridges fairly close together, several bends lead to a weir.
G(W)	The weir has several wooden stakes in it, but can be safely taken through the broken section at its right-hand end.
H(III)	Easy water, and a right-hand bend lead to the 'fish step' rapids. Inspect from the footpath on the right bank. The 'fish steps' are caused by a series of natural angled drops in the river. The rapid starts with a series of standing waves which lead to the three drops, and more rapids. A pool at the bottom becomes washed through in flood conditions.
I(II)	Easier water leads to Patton bridge with the road on the right. After the bridge a left bend brings you to a large pool with a sign saying 'Private Fishing Patton Mill'.
J(III)	From the pool two short rapids follow. Rocks lie hidden below the surface.
K(II)	Open fields on both sides lead to a 1m high man-made square structure. This marks the position of a single strand of barbed wire across the river, at a lethal height.
L(W)	200m from here is a broken weir, once a problem to shoot, but now easier.
M(III)	Below the weir is a long rapid. There are a number of possible lines and it is worth inspecting to choose a good route. A tree half-way down on the left has some low branches. At high water levels 1.5m standing waves form at the bottom, with a large eddy on either side. Just around the corner is an inconspicuous footbridge.
N(II–III)	The rapids are now easier, with several large bends with good eddies. Ivy bridge is soon reached – BEWARE. The bridge is arched, with two smaller arches on the right bank. Just above the bridge three strands of barbed wire cross the river. Portage on the right bank through the arches. Now low branches are the main problem. As you enter a wooded section several streams enter from the left, and the river becomes much wider and deeper.
O(W)	The weir is shortly after the aqueduct, and consists of a vertical drop of about 2m. A large tree has fallen into the river below, on the right side. At low levels the weir can be taken on the far left. In higher water a horrendous boil develops, a certain killer.
P(II–III)	More small rapids follow until a wall is reached, after some distance, on the right. An eddy on the right can be reached before you pass under a bridge. This is Meall bank. Breakout on the right after the bridge, and inspect the falls.

Q(III+)   The falls look natural, but are in part caused by concrete steps. There are a few metal spikes in the concrete, but they should cause no problem if you stay in your boat. The river is split by a large slab of rock. The right channel is narrow and ends in a fall into a stopper, with overhanging rocks on one side. The left channel drops 1.5m into a big stopper with unpredictable manners. Most of the time it grabs your boat, holds you for a second or so and then spits you out (the right way up). This is followed by a second smaller stopper. A breakout on the left is difficult to gain for the less experienced.

R(II)   Fast-flowing but easy water leads to the next fall.

S (III)   A house on the right marks the next rapid. Several routes are possible. In spate a stopper forms across the whole river, but can be taken safely if you paddle hard enough.

T(II–III) The difficult parts are over for a while, and this excellent section provides many places to play. Laverock bridge provides a good place to finish.

U(II)   Easier water follows until a bridge is seen, made of pipes.

V(W)   Upstream from the bridge is an angled weir, which should cause few difficulties.

W(IV)   After you pass under the pipe bridge the river enters a steep narrow section with several drops. The right bank is a garden and therefore inspection should take place from the left bank.

X(W)   A new weir with a small hut on the right bank. At low levels this weir is a good place to practise, as rescues are easy and the stopper not too strong. In flood, however, concrete sides make the stopper closed at both ends. BEWARE.

Y(II)   100m below the weir is Mint bridge. Egress on the right bank, below the bridge, or continue to the confluence with the Kent.

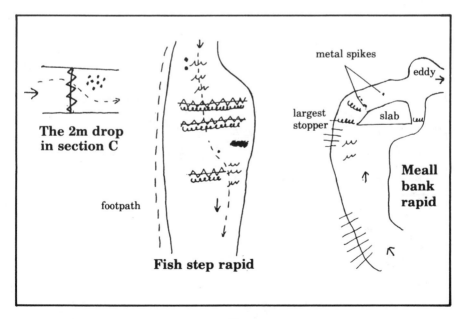

The 2m drop in section C

footpath

Fish step rapid

metal spikes

eddy

largest stopper

slab

Meall bank rapid

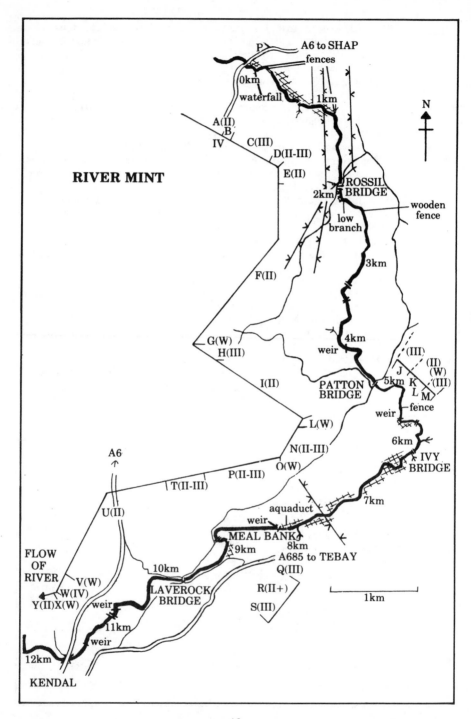

RIVER MINT

P
A6 to SHAP
fences
0km
waterfall
1km
A(II)
B
IV
C(III)
D(II-III)
E(II)
ROSSIL BRIDGE
2km
wooden fence
low branch
3km
F(II)
G(W)
H(III)
4km
weir
(III)
(II)
(W)
(III)
I(II)
J
5km K
L M
PATTON BRIDGE
weir
fence
L(W)
6km
N(II-III)
IVY BRIDGE
O(W)
A6
P(II-III)
7km
T(II-III)
U(II)
aquaduct
weir
MEAL BANK
FLOW OF RIVER
9km
8km
A685 to TEBAY
10km
Q(III)
V(W)
R(II+)
W(IV)
LAVEROCK BRIDGE
S(III)
Y(II)X(W) weir
1km
11km
weir
12km
KENDAL

N

RIVER RAWTHEY

GRADE: III/IV then II/III with one IV

TIME: To straight bridge 1½ hours
To the Lune confluence 2½ hours

DETAILS: LENGTH 14km   HEIGHT LOSS 122m GRADIENT 8.7m/km

INDICATOR: At Sedbergh New bridge there is a layby. If you look down river from the bridge, level with the layby on the right bank of the river is a sandy bank. If this is covered then the river will be a good canoeing level.

ACCESS:

Rawthey bridge (and anywhere downstream for 2km)	713.978
High Wardses bridge	696.960
Straight bridge	678.923
New bridge	665.919
Bridge in Sedbergh	662.913
A683 road bridge	628.896

GENERAL DESCRIPTION

In its higher reaches the Rawthey is little more than a stream. For the first two kilometres the road runs next to the river. A loop in the river brings you to a tricky fall. The rapids are continuous. After Straight bridge the Clough flows into the Rawthey from the left; from here the river is wider and a little easier, but still with some good rapids. The last surprise of the river comes after the old railway viaduct. A two-tier (IV) rapid gives an interesting end to a brilliant river.

DESCRIPTION

A(III)   100m downstream from Rawthey bridge is a large layby. From here access to the river can be gained via a long seal launch down grassy banks if desired. The river is narrow, and the course restricted by vertical projections of rock. There are many small drops.

B(II/III)   The rapids are now easier. There are two awkward falls – one shallow and rocky, next to the bend in the road, the other about 100m above a footbridge.

C(II)   After passing under the footbridge the river flows in a large loop and then cuts back on itself. The water is easy.

D(IV)   Immediately around a tight right loop is a series of rocky outcrops, over which the water falls in three separate falls, one after the other. A difficult rapid.

E(II+)   A short easy stretch leads to a bridge (High Wardes bridge)

F(II)   Many rocks litter the river bed requiring constant manoeuvring to avoid them.

G(III)   On seeing a barn on the left bank, take care. A boulder 1.5m high sits in the middle of the river. It acts as a magnetic rock, and has unseated many paddlers. This is followed by a diagonal stopper across the river.

47

H(II/III)	Easier again but still with many rocks to avoid, the river is excellent. On seeing a bridge, note that the rapid above it is full of sharp rocks. Below the bridge is a small weir made from 20cm pipes. More boulders follow until you see a barn on the right bank. This shows the start of the Rawthey gorge.
I(IV)	The water is more restricted and consequently more powerful. There are four main drops with some difficult rapids in between. At one point a rocky island divides the river and hides the best route from sight. The last fall is the hardest, but is often blocked by trees. The trees that line the gorge have a nasty habit of falling across the river, blocking it completely.
J(III)	An island below is taken left, followed by a sharp left bend and two stoppers.
K(II–III)	The river is now easier and a magnificent waterfall plunges on to the right bank. You soon find yourself in a gorge of conglomerate rock from which escape would be difficult. Fortunately the river is almost flat apart from one narrow section where trees get trapped. At the end of this section is Hebbelthwaite Hall ghyll, conspicuous as it enters the river down a steep culverted channel. Soon Straight Bridge is reached.
L(II)	The river is now wider and the rapids shallow. On the left the river Clough enters. It is worth making the diversion to paddle the last drop on the Clough, only 80m upstream.
M(W)	This is a 1.25m weir offering an unpleasant fish step in the middle, or a bump on to a ledge everywhere else.
N(II)	Around the next corner is a rapid leading under a bridge, closely followed by another weir.
O(W)	A 0.5m wooden affair, the right-hand side of which consists of an outcrop of rock. It is easily taken at the angle between the vertical section and the rocks.
P(III)	Several tight and twisty bends give standing waves and well-defined small eddies.
Q(W)	This weir is broken and has spikes and a reasonable stopper. After the weir is a good grade III rapid which leads to a footbridge.
R(II)	The rapids now get easier as you progress downriver. 500m after passing under the railway viaduct the river drops away steeply and should be inspected from the left bank.
S(IV)	A classic two-tier fall. At lower levels the top fall should be taken left, breaking out, ferry gliding above the bottom drop, to take this on the right. In high water, a much more direct route can be followed but the waves are very big and the stoppers enormous.
T(II/III)	Easier now as the river flows between fields to the final rapid as the river bends left then right to the bridge on the A683, 200m before the Rawthey flows into the Lune.

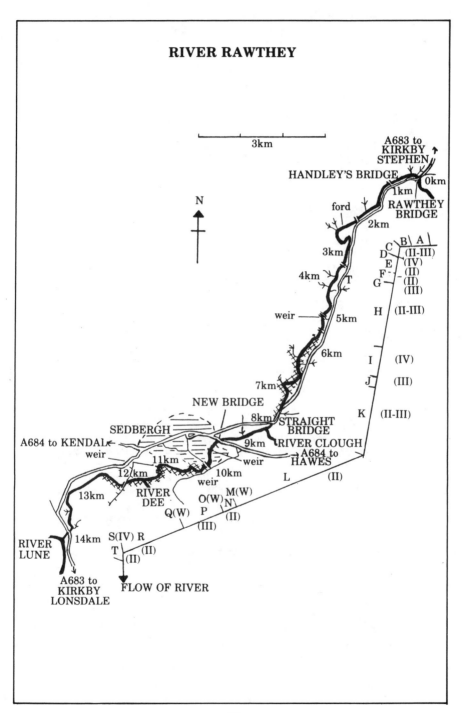

RIVER RAWTHEY

3km

A683 to KIRKBY STEPHEN

HANDLEY'S BRIDGE

0km

N

1km

ford

RAWTHEY BRIDGE

2km

3km

C B A
D (II-III)
E (IV)
F (II)
  (II)
G (III)

4km T

weir 5km H (II-III)

6km I (IV)

7km J (III)

NEW BRIDGE

8km STRAIGHT BRIDGE K (II-III)

SEDBERGH

A684 to KENDAL 9km RIVER CLOUGH
weir A684 to HAWES

11km weir L (II)

12km 10km
weir

13km RIVER DEE M(W)
O(W) N
Q(W) P (II)
(III)

14km S(IV) R
RIVER LUNE T (II)
(II)

A683 to KIRKBY LONSDALE FLOW OF RIVER

49

RIVER ROTHAY

GRADE: II

TIME: 1½ hours

DETAILS: LENGTH 6km   HEIGHT LOSS 90m   GRADIENT 15m/km

INDICATOR: The stepping stones at G.R. 366.056 give a good indication as to the level of the river. In flood they are covered. At medium levels you can get through the stones by tilting your kayak on its side. At low levels you will need to portage.

ACCESS:

Layby on the A591 south of Grasmere	353.065
White Moss car park	349.065
Stepping stones	366.056
Miller bridge	371.045
Rothay weir (opposite hotel; ask here for permission)	371.040
Waterhead hotel on Windermere	376.033

GENERAL DESCRIPTION

The Rothay flows from Grasmere to Windermere, below the slopes of Loughrigg fell. It is popular among novices, and offers a good introduction to river touring. The road is never far away. The river is canoeable at most levels, though some scraping should be expected at low levels. In spate conditions low branches can cause problems in several places.

DESCRIPTION

A(II+)   At the outlet from Grasmere a small weir can be taken anywhere. A footbridge is immediately followed by a 100m rapid which has many small boulders. At the bottom a good eddy can be found on the right.

B(II)   The next section of several bends is made more difficult by the presence of overhanging trees.

C(II)   Three small rapids follow, each followed by a flatter section.

D(II)   The river now widens and becomes shallow. A footbridge will be passed under.

E(I)   Slow water now leads to Rydal water. If you park at White Moss car park, you will start your trip here.

The paddle across Rydal water is pleasant enough, passing Heron island on the way.

F(II)   As you leave Rydal water the banks are again covered with overhanging trees. You pass under a footbridge and the current quickens as you approach Pelter bridge rapid.

G(III)   It is worth inspecting this short but steep rapid from the right bank. It is characterized by hundreds of rocks that litter the whole rapid. A rock-free route is difficult to see. At low levels it is best portaged.

H(II)   Now follows a swift but easy section, with several large breakouts. Rydal beck enters from the left. More of the same follows, until the stepping stones are reached.

I(II) Fast water with occasional large waves, and some trees, especially at G.R. 363.052, lead to Miller bridge after about 15 minutes' paddling. At Miller bridge Stock ghyll enters from the left. A fall at the bottom of this provides an interesting diversion to the main river.

J(II) 100m downstream from Miller bridge bushes infringe both banks of the river. Small rapids lead to Rothay weir. A safe sloping weir with eddies at each side. This is a popular place to stop and play. If you are to stop here, you should ask for permission to use the car park at the hotel opposite.

K(II) More easy water leads to the Ambleside-Coniston road bridge. After this the flow becomes gradually slower as the confluence with the Brathay is reached, followed by Windermere.

RIVER ROTHAY

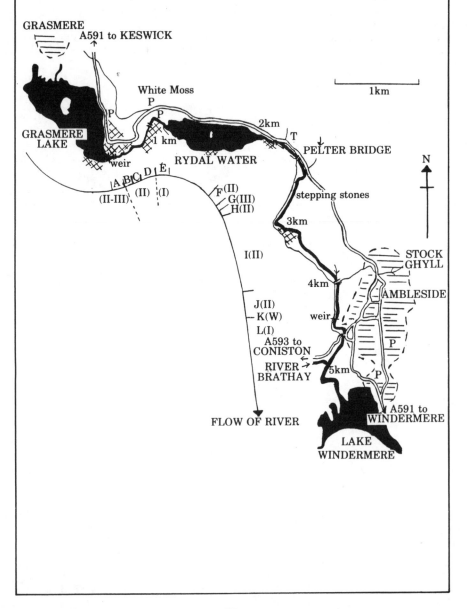

GRASMERE

A591 to KESWICK

White Moss

P

P

P

2km

T

GRASMERE
LAKE

1 km

PELTER BRIDGE

N

weir

RYDAL WATER

A B C D E

(II-III)   (II)   (I)

F (II)

G (III)

H (II)

stepping stones

3km

I (II)

STOCK
GHYLL

AMBLESIDE

4km

J (II)

K (W)

L (I)

weir

A593 to
CONISTON

P

RIVER
BRATHAY

5km

P

A591 to
WINDERMERE

FLOW OF RIVER

LAKE
WINDERMERE

1km

RIVER SPRINT

GRADE: IV

TIME: 2 hours

DETAILS: LENGTH 8km · HEIGHT LOSS 108m · GRADIENT 13.5m/km

INDICATOR: If it is possible to paddle around the bend below Sprint bridge at G.R. 513.960 without scraping the river will be high enough to paddle. See section P also.

ACCESS:

Road to Docker farm (limited parking)	509.015
Across a field just south of Garnett bridge	523.992
Gurnall bridge	521.975
Sprint bridge	513.960
Footpath/road by river Kent at the confluence	508.953

GENERAL DESCRIPTION

The Sprint flows from Longsleddale to the river Kent just below Burneside. In condition it gives one of the best white water trips in Cumbria, with five difficult sections and continuous rapids between. At Cocks Close (521.997) is a difficult rapid on tight double S-bends which cannot be portaged because of the thick vegetation on one bank and a house on the other. This rapid should be inspected before being attempted. The Sprint is rarely paddled except by a few local enthusiasts, and even then most start below the fall at Garnett bridge.

DESCRIPTION

A(II)   The bridge at Docker Nook farm provides a good starting place, though no official permission has been gained. Please park sensibly on the roadside, not on the farm track

B(II)   The first two kilometres provide a nice warm-up, being mostly flat with small rapids. On seeing a house ahead with four uneven windows on its top level, prepare yourself for the S-bends.

C(IV)   The S-bends are littered with rocks of all sizes; it is difficult to paddle these without some banging, as each chute is guarded at its base by a rock. The river bends to the right, most of the water hugging the left bank. A sharp left turn needs skilful manoeuvre to stay in the current, and then somehow you need to gain the left side from the right with little room to do this. A fall into a small pool is followed by a right then left manoeuvre to finish this difficult stretch. Easier rapids follow.

D(W)   This weir should be treated with care, but is normally suitable to shoot.

E(III)   More rapids lead to Garnett bridge.

F(IV)   The river narrows under the arched bridge. The route is obvious. Start right at the first fall, moving left over a nasty-looking rock directly upstream of the bridge. This line will give you the correct route for the 3m-wide gorge below, which you will pass through very quickly.

53

G(III)	Now easier but still continuous, if small, III follows. After a left bend a good eddy is to be found with adjacent standing waves. More of the same follows until you reach a tight bend to the right which you cannot see round. In fact this bend provides no canoeing difficulties (but beware of fallen trees). 200–300m down a long straight section brings the next fall.
H(IV)	Look for a boulder covered in moss 2m from the right bank. On seeing this get out on the left and inspect. A classic fall 3m high and 10m long into a deep pool. Narrow at first, and a wave half-way down which has a habit of capsizing boats to the left. The stopper will cause no problems because of your immense speed. A portage is possible on the left.
I(III)	A few small rapids lead almost immediately to another section best inspected from the left.
J(III+)	From the bank the route looks easy and straight, but in fact is rather twisty. A harmless-looking folding wave half-way down will attempt to loop most boats, and cause a fair number to roll or bail out. 20m below this wave is a fall of about 1m with a rock in the middle at the top. The left side is best, and be prepared for another near loop.
K(II–III)	Now easy water leads under Gurnall bridge. Downstream small rapids lead to a right bend and a loop in the river around Holme house farm on the left.
L(W)	After the farm a right bend holds a broken weir. Beware of trapped branches and old stakes. The right-hand side of the weir is broken: this is the route usually followed.
M(III)	An excellent stretch over rock shelves leads to Oak bank on the left. After a left bend a tree stands in the middle of the river. Just below is Sprint mill falls.
N(IV)	Sprint mill falls. Here a good drop in the river provides an interesting problem. The fall is normally taken half sideways a few metres from the right bank, moving left and then right to finish through a slot in a rocky ridge that spans the river. In high flood large cushions and stoppers form on this fall making it a formidable problem. Just above the pipe bridge are large eddies (see plan).
O(III)	Below the pipe bridge is an angled stopper, which can be quite big. The next bend is narrow and awkward, with low boughs to add to the difficulties. On the right is Sprint mill cottage, so inspection must be done from the left bank. This section ends with a drop under a small footbridge with bushes hanging into the river.
P(W)	The weir can be easily taken in the centre. There are gauges at this weir. A level of 0.6 on the gauge above the weir is considered to be the minimum level for canoeing. (This level will involve much banging on rocks.)
Q	The river eases to Sprint bridge – a good place to egress.
R(II)	A small but easy series of bends follow leading to a large pool. Finally a canalized but fast-flowing section leads to the river Kent.

Double S-bends

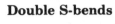

Cocks close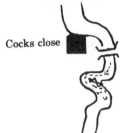

Garnett bridge

Sprint mill falls

Broken weir

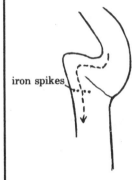

iron spikes

Sprint mill
cottages

pipe bridge

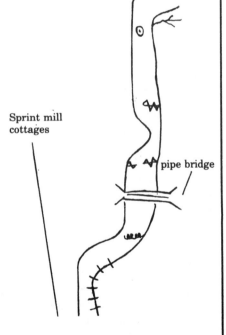

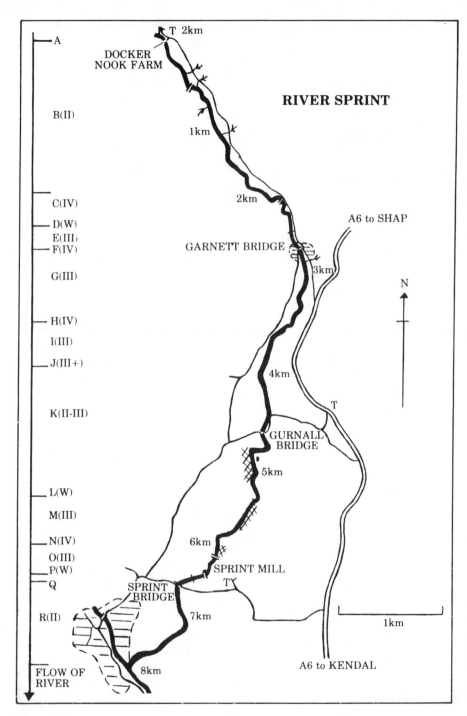

RIVER SPRINT

T 2km
DOCKER
NOOK FARM

A6 to SHAP

GARNETT BRIDGE

3km

N

GURNALL
BRIDGE

5km

SPRINT MILL
T

SPRINT
BRIDGE

1km

A6 to KENDAL

A
B(II)
C(IV)
D(W)
E(III)
F(IV)
G(III)
H(IV)
I(III)
J(III+)
K(II-III)
L(W)
M(III)
N(IV)
O(III)
P(W)
Q
R(II)
FLOW OF
RIVER

TROUTBECK

GRADE: Car park at the start – Troutbeck bridge III/IV
Troutbeck bridge – lake Windermere II

TIME: 45 mins to Troutbeck bridge.   1 hour to Windermere

DETAILS: LENGTH 4km   HEIGHT LOSS 112m GRADIENT 28m/km

INDICATOR: If you can float down the first 50m without scraping on rocks the river will be paddleable. In general the deeper the river is here, the harder it will be lower down.

ACCESS: Car park next to the river 100m south of Troutbeck church 413.027
Troutbeck bridge (next to the garage forecourt)   403.003
Millerground landing on Windermere   402.987

GENERAL DESCRIPTION

The river Troutbeck drains the Troutbeck valley into lake Windermere. Owing to its small catchment area it rarely reaches big flood conditions, though it will have enough water to be canoeable after heavy rain, rising and falling in a matter of hours. Despite this the Troutbeck is an excellent trip. Anyone attempting it without full confidence in their ability to manoeuvre their kayak quickly and efficiently is advised to go elsewhere or suffer the consequences.

If you are to finish at Troutbeck bridge then please ask permission at the garage to leave your car – they are usually most helpful.

It is essential to inspect the gorge under the pipeline for trees, as it is entered blind from the river. This is best done from the pipeline which is reached by steps from the road at G.R. 407.015.

Trees often block parts of the river, sometimes completely, and so care is essential at all times.

DESCRIPTION

A(II)   The car park provides an easy place to launch. The first section is pleasant, and provides a chance to become accustomed to the speed of the river, which can be very quick.

B(III)   After a few bends an island is reached. This should be taken to the right, as a low bridge over the left channel is likely to decapitate you. Whilst rounding the island you will meet a tree growing in the river: this is easily avoided. Then a bump – a rock hidden under the water where the two channels meet.

C(III)   Now continuous rapids follow lined by overhanging branches. When you see a wooded hill/bank ahead, a large breakout on the left, before a right bend, should be gained.

D(IV)   The first gorge section follows. A steep rocky rapid leads to several small drops, as the river bends sharply left. The last fall should be taken to the left since it twists as it falls. Now you can see ahead but skill is required to reach the pipe bridge safely. A rest can be had on the left below the pipes some 20m above.

E(III/IV)	Large standing waves lead to a right bend where confused water flows more rapidly around large rocks holding stoppers form at high water levels. Much skill is needed for a successful descent. This continues for about 100m. A house on the left is opposite a small rocky island with a difficult route past it.
F(III)	More standing waves follow to a left bend which in turn is followed by shallower water; this last section often has fallen trees. Soon two steep rapids with deep water are passed; these lead to a weir.
G(W)	The weir is large but angled, but the difficulties lie first in the fact that it is angled across the river on a bend, and secondly in its attraction to large tree stumps. Immediately following the weir is a bouncy, aerated rapid with large waves and shallow rocks at its bottom.
H(II)	At last a chance to relax, if only for 100m.
I(W)	This should be taken in the middle aiming to the left of a narrow part 10m on. The weir itself should cause no problems.
J(IV)	The next 50m is an exhilarating 'canoeists' bobsleigh run' finishing with a tricky manoeuvre to gain a tongue on a 1m drop through an angled stopper.
	Now the river drops steeply. A large boiling stopper in the middle of the river must first be negotiated. Now a series of steps, each with a stopper, follow. As you descend try to move to the right to take a roller-coaster ride through the final stoppers and standing waves below a high wall on the right. This section can be inspected from the east bank, access to which is gained through a factory yard opposite the garage at Troutbeck bridge. (NB There is no official right of way here.)
K(II)	Easier water leads to Troutbeck bridge where a small stopper forms over a step in the concrete bed. Egress on the left bank at the garage.
L(II)	The flow is still swift and there are many small boulders to avoid.
M(I)	Now the difficulties are over and you will be washed down to lake Windermere. A paddle of about 1km following the bank to the left will lead to Millerground landing – a chance to reflect on the trip.

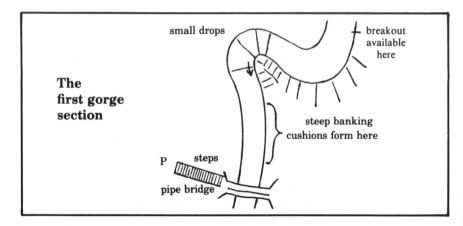

The
first gorge
section

small drops

breakout
available
here

steep banking
cushions form here

P   steps

pipe bridge

RIVER TROUTBECK

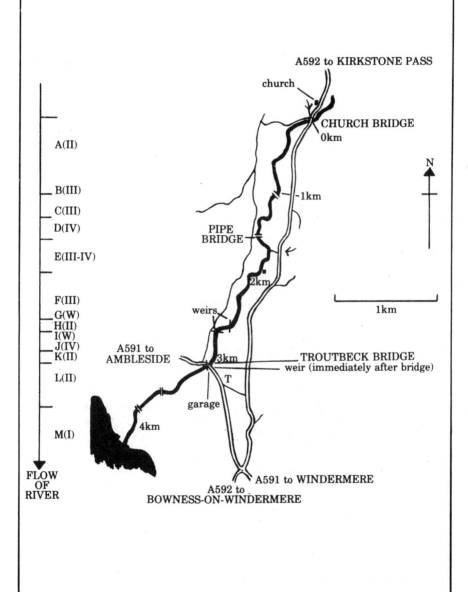

A592 to KIRKSTONE PASS

church

CHURCH BRIDGE
0km

A(II)

N

B(III)

C(III)

D(IV)

E(III-IV)

PIPE
BRIDGE

1km

2km

F(III)

G(W)

H(II)

I(W)

J(IV)

K(II)

L(II)

weirs

1km

A591 to
AMBLESIDE

3km

TROUTBECK BRIDGE
weir (immediately after bridge)

T

garage

M(I)

4km

FLOW
OF
RIVER

A591 to WINDERMERE

A592 to
BOWNESS-ON-WINDERMERE

RIVER GRETA (Ingleton)

GRADE: II/III

TIME: 2 hours

DETAILS: LENGTH 10km   HEIGHT LOSS 100m   GRADIENT 10m/km

INDICATOR: At the A65 roadbridge at Ingleton if the water is deep enough to paddle on, the river will be canoeable.

ACCESS:

Ingleton (parking difficult)	695.735
Ingleton (east bank by viaduct)	694.732
A65 road bridge (park in village)	689.727
Burton in Lonsdale (South bank)	656.720
Greta bridge	611.726
Gressingham bridge (on Lune)	582.697

GENERAL DESCRIPTION

The Greta takes the water from the West side of Ingleborough and Kingsdale from the river Doe and Kingsdale beck. These two rivers meet above the viaduct to form the Greta. The river rises and falls quickly after heavy rain. It provides an exciting run in high water.

DESCRIPTION

A(III)   From the minor road to Kingsdale access to the river can be gained. The bed is steep and strewn with small boulders.

B(W)   As you reach the viaduct the river is split by one of the viaduct supports. Most water flows through the left arch. There is a choice of routes. Next to the support in the middle of the river is a easy angled slope of 1.5m leading to a stopper closed at both ends. This is followed by a flat pool and a vertical drop of 1 metre which is blocked by boulders in places. The alternative is to hug the left bank and take the weir by a series of fish steps, 7 in all, which follow in quick succession.

C(II/III)   As the river leaves Ingleton it flows through open fields over a variety of shingle rapids and bed rock shelves. Eddies are well defined and large. In high water several rapids produce large standing waves especially by a caravan site at G.R. 672.718.

D(III+)   200 metres above the bridge at Burton in Lonsdale is an excellent access point. The Bridge has two arches, both of which support stoppers that are usually no problem. In fact the stopper of the right arch is a fine play wave with eddies on either side. Below the bridge are a series of bedding plane ledges which can give an exciting ride at high water.

E(III)   The river now enters a wooded section and has a few interesting rapids. In between are easier sections. The main difficulties end with a fall of 1.5 metres which is quickly followed by a rocky reef which can produce some unpredictable water.

F(II)   Easier water leads over shingle rapids to the egress on the outside of the bend (right bank) just above Greta bridge. Or you can continue on to the confluence with the Lune and egress after another 4km.

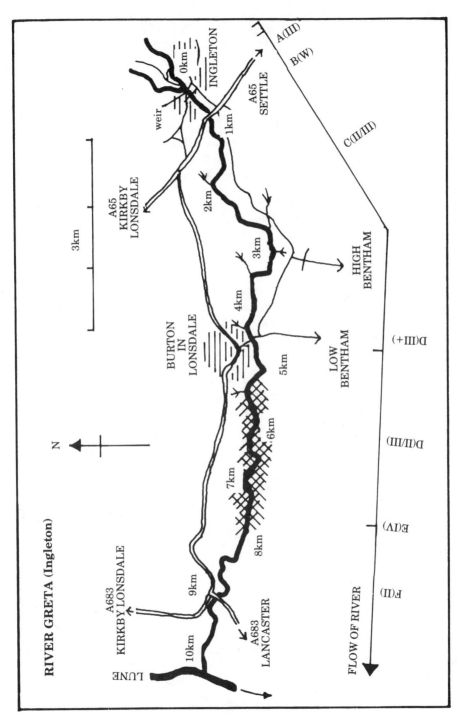

RIVER GRETA (Ingleton)

RIVER WENNING

GRADE: II with some more difficult weirs

TIME: 3½ to 4 hours

DETAILS: LENGTH 19km   HEIGHT LOSS 132m   GRADIENT 6.9m/km

INDICATOR: In general the level of the river can be gauged by examining the flow at the bridge by the Punch Bowl Inn in Low Bentham.

ACCESS:	Clapham	744.692
	Clapham station	733.678
	Road bridge	692.682
	High Bentham bridge	668.687
	Low Bentham bridge	646.693
	Wennington bridge	617.700
	Road bridge (no official access)	610.693
	Hornby bridge	585.684

GENERAL DESCRIPTION
The Wenning flows from the limestone on the east and south sides of Ingleborough. There is a delay of about 12 hours after heavy rain before the river rises since most of the water emerges from underground cave systems.

DESCRIPTION
A(II)   The stretch from Clapham to Clapham station is rarely canoed and has no real problems.

B(II)   After the bridge at Clapham station the river meanders and overhanging bushes may catch the less skilled.

C(W)   Several weirs of about 0.3m span the river, beware of iron stakes hiding in stoppers.

D(II)   Pleasant scenery and the odd steeper rapid lead through High Bentham and on until the river bends to the left.

E(III)   A reef crosses the river being about 1m on the right and smallest on the left. The river bends to the right immediately after the reef.

F(II)   Easy water soon leads to two weirs.

G(W)   The first weir is 1m high and can be taken easily. The second weir is about 4m and angled. It is most easily taken on the far right in one drop, or with more difficulty by a series of steps on the left.

H(II)   Above the two bridges of Low Bentham lie a pipeline with metal supports. Care should be taken as logs jam on these supports and can block the whole river.

I(W)   Under the bridge at Wennington is an easy angled sloping 2m weir. The stopper has a bit of a kick and the following wave can also cause problems. A flat section leads to the next weir. This can be paddled anywhere. This is a small weir that will hold you more than you think.

J(I)   More easy water leads to another weir.

K(W)   This weir is horse shoe shaped and can be taken anywhere.

L(I)   The river crosses open fields to the town of Hornby.

M(W)   A large angled-weir can be safely taken in a number of places. Egress on the left bank by the bridge.

N(I)   More easy water leads to the river Lune.

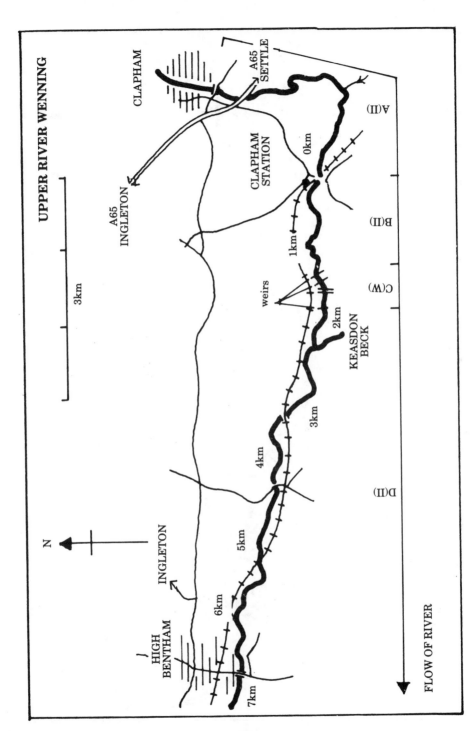

UPPER RIVER WENNING

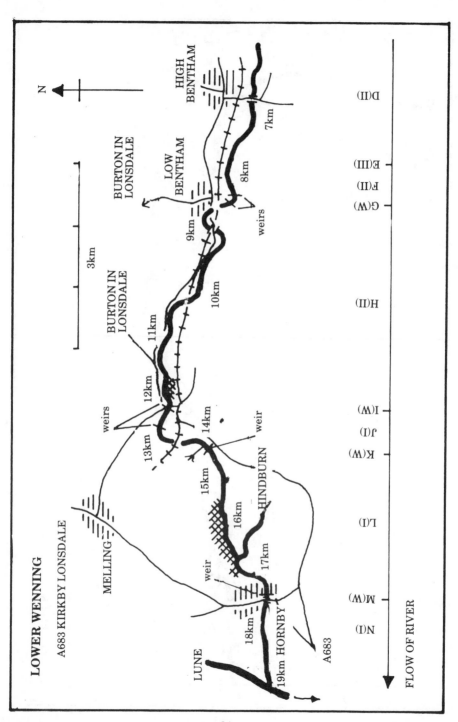

LOWER WENNING

A683 KIRKBY LONSDALE

N

FLOW OF RIVER

3km

BURTON IN LONSDALE

BURTON IN LONSDALE

LOW BENTHAM

HIGH BENTHAM

MELLING

HINDBURN

LUNE

A683

HORNBY

weirs

weirs

weirs

weir

weir

7km
8km
9km
10km
11km
12km
13km
14km
15km
16km
17km
18km
19km

D(II)
E(III)
F(II)
G(W)
H(II)
I(W)
J(I)
K(W)
L(I)
M(W)
N(I)

RIVER HINDBURN

GRADE: II to IV with one fall of V

TIME: 1½ hours

DETAILS: LENGTH 8km   HEIGHT LOSS 90m   GRADIENT 11.3m/km

INDICATOR: Looking upstream from the bridge at G.R. 613.676 plenty of water should be flowing over the visable fall from bank to bank.

ACCESS:

Road bend	649.641
Bridge	635.669
Bridge	613.676
Bridge and layby	604.680

GENERAL DESCRIPTION

The Hindburn is only paddleable after heavy rain and quickly loses its water. The main rapids are caused by angled bedding planes and their ends.

DESCRIPTION

A(II)   The river soon eases into easy rapids.

B(IV)   After only a few bends steep bedding planes are reached, fast and shallow you quickly build up speed to punch through the stoppers at the bottom. In high water be prepared to brace on the stoppers (which may be large), until they quickly move you to their weakness and let you go, exhilerating stuff. Each slide is followed by a pool before the next slide, there are three in all.

C(III)   Some pleasant grade III water leads past wooded banks and the odd cliff to a road bridge.

D(II)   Now easier you should look for a bridge and land above it, for after this stopping is difficult above the grade V fall.

E(V)   This an intimidating three teir fall that drops 4m in all.

F(III/IV)   Below the fall are several drops of 1m to 1.5m and a few playable III's.

G(II)   After the next bridge the water is easier to a small weir above the last bridge where egress is made on the left bank.

H(I)   Easier still the Hindburn soon flows into the Wenn: ıg.

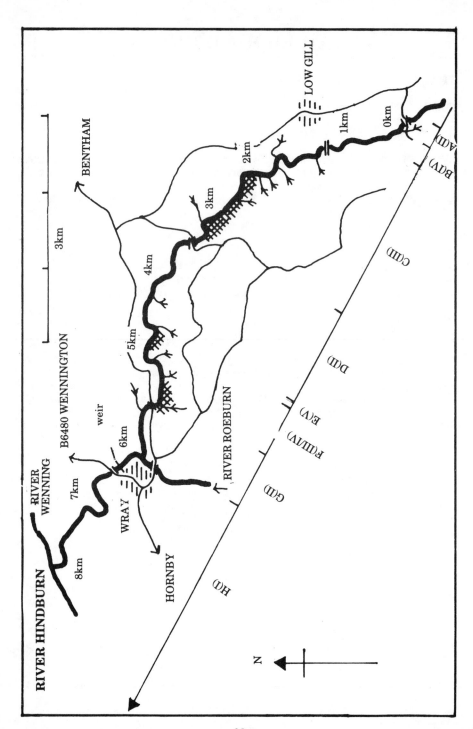

RIVER HINDBURN

RIVER WENNING

BENTHAM

3km

B6480 WENNINGTON

WRAY

weir

7km

6km

5km

4km

3km

2km

1km

0km

8km

HORNBY

RIVER ROEBURN

LOW GILL

A(III)

B(IV)

C(III)

D(II)

E(V)

F(II/IV)

G(III)

H(I)

N

66

RIVER ROEBURN

GRADE: III with one IV

TIME: 75 minutes

DETAILS: LENGTH 4km   HEIGHT LOSS 100m   GRADIENT 25m/km

INDICATOR: If there is enough water to be able to easily pass under the bridge at 605.675 the river will be worth paddling.

ACCESS: Bridge   601.637
              Bridge   605.675
              Bridge (on Hindburn)   604.680

GENERAL DESCRIPTION
This is a small catchment river that requires heavy rain to make it canoeable. It is remarkably consistent at its grade.

DESCRIPTION
A(III)   The river is easily gained from a small layby just by the roadbridge, it is not suitable for minibuses. The rapids start as they mean to go on, with small brakouts and continuous small boulders. After about 1km a large stream enters on the right down a series of falls in a small gorge, following this is a 400m stretch of slides and stoppers. This is followed by slightly easier rapids which pass through open fields in a series of bends then a long straight. (Beware, 1 wire fence.)

B(IV)   At the end of the straight the river is harder. This can be recognised by the flow against a small cliff. Here follows an S-bend and a fall of 2m which is taken by a steep chute on the right of the boulder. (Difficult to inspect.)

C(II+)   Now easier the river is vegetated in places and fallen trees may block the river. The best egress is just below the road bridge in the village of Wray or continue to the next bridge on the Hindburn.

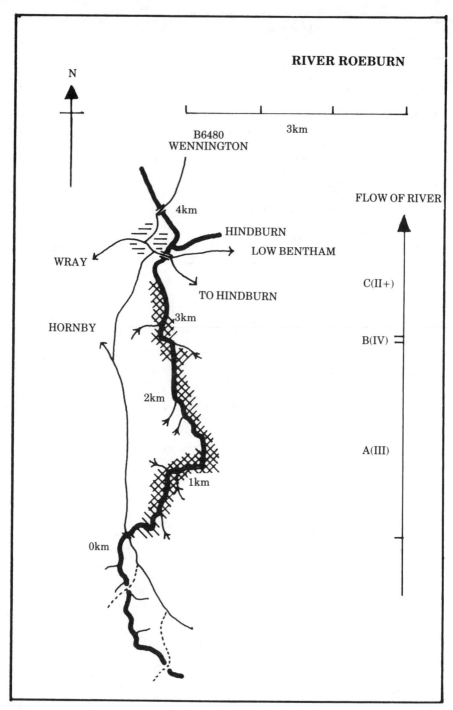

RIVER ROEBURN

N

3km

B6480
WENNINGTON

FLOW OF RIVER

4km

HINDBURN

LOW BENTHAM

WRAY

C(II+)

TO HINDBURN

HORNBY

3km

B(IV)

2km

A(III)

1km

0km

Appendix A

Other less popular rivers

The following is a selection of the smaller or less paddled rivers and streams in Cumbria. There are many more, most needing heavy rain to make them viable; they are there awaiting the explorer.

BORROW BECK (II–IV; 8km; 21m/km)

Borrow beck drains the south side of the Shap fells, and needs very heavy rain to bring it into condition. Access is only possible at the start and finish. Start at G.R. 039.553 on the A6 8 miles north of Kendal. Park in a layby with a telephone.

The river runs across open moors, the only habitation being two isolated farms. At first the river is shallow with many boulders. After 2km a bridge will be reached near a farm. The valley sides gradually steepen. A second bridge signals the start of more difficult rapids. Here it is a grade III+ to the finish, with some sections of IV, including a fall (V) of 2.5m which most paddlers will want to portage. Egress is at G.R. 611.010 at a layby on the A685, 2 miles south of Shap. On downstream is a weir underneath a motorway bridge. This is followed by a small bridge, and the confluence with the river Lune after a further 100m. Borrow beck has continuous rapids from start to finish, with not one section of flat water along its entire length, thus making it unique amongst Cumbrian rivers.

LITTLE LANGDALE BECK (mostly II/III, 2 portages; 3.5km; 11.5m/km)

Easiest access is from the ford at G.R. 316.029. This can be reached via a narrow lane (unsuitable for trailers) from the A593 past Stang End farm or from Little Langdale. At the ford is a bridge; the first obstacle is a fence – care needed – portage. Small rapids with a few larger ones and large breakouts can be found in the main. A sharp left bend leads to a small weir. Portage on the right, for below is Colwith force: an impressive sight, the drops being roughly 2m, 3m, 2m and 8m into a deep pool. Below this the river bends to the right and becomes III, with an interesting fall past a huge boulder. Following this is less difficult water, eventually to a road bridge G.R. 330.030, and 1km more to Elter water.

STOCK GHYLL (IV–V; 1km; 50m/km)

Stock Ghyll flows through Ambleside and is better known for the waterfalls at its top end. It is still in condition two or three times a year, and has had very few descents. It has big, continuous rapids and stoppers, with much confused water. This, combined with no breakouts and low bridges, attracts canoeists with a death wish, lots of skill and just as much luck.

Stock Ghyll flows into the river Rothay in Ambleside park. Here an interesting fall can provide an added bonus to a trip down the Rothay.

CUNSEY BECK (II(IV); 3km; 10m/km)

A narrow stream flowing from Esthwaite water to Windermere. Flat in many places and crossed by barbed wire in several places, combined with tight bends and low branches, make this a rarely canoed river. The last section, a gorge graded at IV, is usually blocked by many fallen trees which would need to be cleared.

CLOUGH (II–IV; 12km; 17m/km; steeper in the lower section)
The Clough flows from Garsdale head to the Rawthey above Sedbergh. The upper reaches rarely receive enough water to make them worth canoeing. The A684 follows the river for most of its length; normally it is a matter of driving up the road until you think it is worth getting on. The upper parts flow over limestone beddings, and several 1m-and 2m-drops are to be found. Trees are a problem in places. Many small streams join the Clough, thus increasing its flow in the lower reaches.

After the road bridge at G.R. 713.907 (New bridge) the river leaves the road and flows down several narrow gorges. Easy at first, several drops of 1.5m and 2m are to be found. A narrow part followed by deep pools and some undercut rocks can be inspected from the bridge at G.R. 699.913. The next section is very narrow and steep, and is very boily at high water levels, normally IV. From here to the finish is never a dull moment, with some intricate and steep falls, rapids and a weir. The final fall is about 2m and leads directly to the river Rawthey.

DEE (II–V; 1 portage;   13km; 14m/km)
The Dee flows down Dentdale to join the Rawthey below Sedbergh. It is similar in nature to the Clough. Trees can be a problem. A'B'road runs beside the river in its upper parts.

The upper river is continuously steep with few breakouts. The water is channeled in places as it flows over limestone bedding planes. Several 1m+ falls will be found. Around Ibbeth Peril cave G.R. 741.864 and for 1km downstream is a small limestone gorge. There are 4 large falls, the largest being 4m. This section is very dangerous at high water, with few tight breakouts and at least one portage (the third fall). Some of the water flows down Ibbeth Peril cave thus taking some volume from the gorge. This water re enters after the gorge. From here to the road bridge at Dent G.R. 708.872 is grade I/II. Below this is 8km of grade I with a series of grade III rapids leading to the confluence with the Rawthey. Needs heavy rain to be canoeable.

YEWDALE BECK (II–III; 3km; 16m/km)
This river flows into Coniston water from the north. The A593 is nearby in the middle section. Again needing high rainfall to bring it into condition. Access can be gained at several places, none of them easy. Trees may block the river, and fences can cause problems.

IRT, EHEN, BLENG
The Irt flows out of Wastwater to the Irish sea.
The Ehen flows out of Ennerdale water to the Irish sea.
The Bleng flows from a remote valley between the two above lakes into the Irt. The Irt and Ehen are predominantly flat water rivers. Access problems occur on both rivers, and canoeing is not officially allowed on the Ehen. The Bleng has a reasonable gradient and could offer canoeing potential.

CALDEW (II; 5½km; 10m/km)
The Caldew flows north along the slopes of Carrock Fell in the north of the county. Never difficult but with the constant possibility of a tree across the river and excellent scenery give this river interest. It is rarely paddled. Suggested trip G.R. 360.342 to G.R. 344.388.

70

GELT (II–IV; 2 portages 8.5km; 15.9m/km)
The Gelt lies to the S.E. of Carlisle, and drains Geltdale. It is a steep bouldery stream in its upper reaches with the occasional more confined part. It is over grown by bushes in places. Lower down it flows through small sandstone gorges, notably at the B6413 road bridge where the first portage is found and in Gelt woods where the river is very channeled and many logs lie in the river. The best egress is at the end of Gelt woods (Low Gelt Bridge). Suggested trip 560.551 or 571.541 to 520.592.

IRTHING (II with some III/IV; 1 portage; 13km; 9.2m/km)
The Irthing drains a large area of moors to the N.E. of Carlisle. The river is mostly grade II with a 2m fall (IV) at G.R. 685.730 and a 6m fall, portage, at G.R. 638.696. Below the second fall is a gorge of about 1km with grade III/IV rapids. At the end of the gorge sulphur may be smelt at a hot spring. Finish at Gilsland Bridge. Suggested trip 678.743 to 633.663.

RIBBLE (III(V); 2.5km; 20m/km)
The best section on the Ribble for the white water enthusiast is the short section from Helwith bridge to Stainforth force, to the south of Horton in Ribblesdale. Good water levels are needed and some of the rapids are very steep being blocked with an assortment of boulders and bedrock. Unfortunately at high enough water levels to make the section good Stainforth force becomes very dangerous. It is a fall of several levels the last of which holds a stopper closed at both ends by small limestone cliffs. Rescue of a swimmer can be difficult. At lower levels the fall is a little easier but should be treated with care.

Downstream to Settle are a few weirs and easier water. The river continues in a similar manner to the sea at Preston (about 50km).

The recommended section can be paddled in about 25 minutes. (G.R. 811.695 to 823.661).

Appendix B

1 These rivers are less frequently paddled and there is no reported objection to canoeing:
CLOUGH, DEE, LITTLE LANGDALE BECK, MINT, SPRINT, TROUTBECK, UPPER KENT.
2 These rivers have vague access agreements, but are normally paddled at all times of the year, water level permitting:
BRATHAY, GREAT LANGDALE BECK, ROTHAY, UPPER DERWENT.
3 These rivers have no access agreement but there is usually no objection to canoeing outside the fishing season:
ESK, LUNE.
4 These rivers have an agreement to be canoed outside the fishing season and at certain other times in the fishing season (including access and egress points):
EDEN, GRETA (KESWICK), MIDDLE DERWENT.
5 These rivers have agreements for canoeing outside of the fishing season only:
CRAKE, DUDDON.
6 These rivers have only specific days on which canoeing is permitted:
LEVEN.
7 These rivers have no agreement, but permission can usually be obtained by request to the major land owner:
EAMONT, LOWTHER.
8 These rivers need to be approached delicately in order to secure canoeing for the future, i.e. be polite, no large groups:
RAWTHEY, LOWER DERWENT, LOWER KENT.

In the fishing season the following rivers are heavily fished, and a full trip of the river is not usually possible without being asked to leave the river:
KENT, LUNE, DUDDON, CRAKE, GRETA, EDEN (except by agreement), DERWENT (lower).

Details of access agreements and current situations are available from the local access officers of the British Canoe Union. No details of these are given as personnel change at short notice.

Please report any incidents good or otherwise to the L.A.O. with names of the parties involved.

Increasing pressure on the rivers in Cumbria by canoeists has lead to the access situation on several rivers deteriorating. Large groups and irresponsible individuals being the main culprits. You can do your bit by avoiding doing the following:
Driving across fields and crops
Damaging hedges, walls, and fences
Disturbing wildlife
Leaving gates open
Blocking access to fields and private dwellings
Annoying local inhabitants
but also try to do the following:
Change discretely
Be polite to other river users and local residents

Drive slowly through small villages
Stick to access agreements where they exist
Leave signs where they are put

Appendix C

Maps

The grid references are taken from ordnance survey maps. A list of the maps consulted for each river is given below.

RIVER	MAP(S)
BRATHAY	A, D, K
COCKER	A, C, H
CRAKE	A, E, M
DERWENT	A, D, H
DUDDON	A, E, I
EAMONT	A, D, J
EDEN	A, B, J
ESK	A, E, I
GREAT LANGDALE BECK	A, D, I, K
GRETA	A, D, H
KENT	A, F, K
LEVEN	A, E, M
LOWTHER	A, D, J
LUNE	F, L, O
MINT	A, F, K
RAWTHEY	G, L
ROTHAY	A, D, K
SPRINT	A, F, K
TROUTBECK	A, D, K

CLOUGH	L, N
DEE	L, N
LITTLE LANGDALE BECK	A, D, K
BORROW BECK	K, O
STOCK GHYLL	A, D, K
YEWDALE BECK	A, F, K
WENNING	F, G
GRETA (Ingleton)	F, G
HINDBURN	F
ROEBURN	F
CALDEW	D
GELT	B
IRTHING	B

O.S. 1" Tourist map		A	
O.S. 1 : 50000 map	86	B	Haltwhistle
	89	C	Whitehaven and Workington
	90	D	Penrith and Keswick
	96	E	Barrow-in-Furness
	97	F	Kendal and Lancaster
	98	G	Wenslevdale and Wharfedale
O.S. 1 : 25000 map	N.W.	H	Lake District
	S.W.	I	Lake District
	N.E.	J	Lake District
	S.E.	K	Lake District
	SD 69/79	L	Sedbergh and Baugh Fell
	SD 28/38	M	Broughton-in-Furness and Newby Bridge
	The 3 peaks	N	
O.S. 1 : 50000	91	O	Appleby

A few notes on sea canoeing around the Cumbrian coast

Cumbria is bounded to the south by Morecambe bay, to the north by the Solway firth and to the west by the Irish sea.

Morecambe bay

At low tide most of Morecambe bay consists of large expanses of mud flats. This makes any prolonged trip not worth considering. Some local canoeists paddle on the Crake/Leven estuary around high tide. Over Greenodd sands a few miles down the estuary is the Leven viaduct, where rough water can sometimes be found.

The Kent estuary at Arnside is of more interest, especially on spring tides. There is a tidal bore in this estuary at spring tides. It can vary from nothing, commonly a few inches and occasionally a foot or more. If you set off from the promenade at Arnside, at least 2½ hours before high tide, you should be able to pick it up and surf it a mile or so back to Arnside. The size of the bore seems to be affected by the size of the tide, the strength and direction of the wind, and the volume of water coming down the river Kent.

The railway viaduct at Arnside has about fifty arches. As the tide rushes between them it produces very rough and variable water. One-metre standing waves are not uncommon. The water is constantly changing, and very powerful. Small boils and whirlpools add to the excitement.

Irish sea

The most adventurous trip here is the open crossing to the isle of Man. A trip of about 35 miles and for the expert only.

The coast itself is uninspiring except for the cliffs at St Bees. The trip from here to Whitehaven (and back) is probably the most enjoyable. Other trips can be made starting at or finishing at the following places, listed south to north: Walney island (Barrow), Silecroft, Ravenglass, St Bees, Whitehaven, Maryport, the coast to Silloth. Much of this consists of low-lying, grassy sand-dunes.

Surfing: The three best places to surf are St Bees, Silecroft and Walney island. All of these get the best surf when the wind blows from the west or south-west. Walney seems to be the best bet if the wind blows from the south.

Walney – large open beach, with small pebbles and a large grassy area above the beach. Plenty of parking space.

Silecroft – large open beach consisting of a flat sandy lower part and a steep sand/pebbly upper part. This has the effect of increasing the size of the waves as the tide comes in. At high tide the waves tend to dump, badly if the surf is big. Large parking area and toilets at the top of the beach.

St Bees – a narrower beach bounded by rocks to the right. The top of the beach is made from large pebbles which are kept in place by wooden groins. These are a hazard to surf canoeing at high tide. St Bees probably has the best surf. Car park and village at the top of the beach.

Solway firth

Strong tides on the ebb and flood occur in the Solway firth. Higher up a large area of sand banks is exposed at low tide. There are only a few suitable access points. The Solway is not widely canoed, though there are undoubtedly some worthwhile trips to be done. There are several places where fishing nets are strung between poles; these should be avoided at all costs.